I0223106

CULTIVATING

Homespun Essays
from Beech Tree Lane

© 2020 Dianne Poston Owens

All rights reserved.

No part of this publication in print or in electronic format may be reproduced, stored in a retrieval system, or transmitted in any form or by any means, electronic, mechanical, photocopying, recording, or otherwise without the prior written permission of the publisher.

The scanning, uploading, and distribution of this book without permission is a theft of the author's intellectual property. If you would like permission to use material from the book (other than for review purposes), please contact info@bublish.com. Thank you for your support of the author's rights.

Design and Distribtuion by Bublish, Inc.

ISBN: 978-1-64704-215-8 (hardback)
ISBN: 978-1-64704-214-1 (paperback)
ISBN: 978-1-64704-213-4 (eBook)

CULTIVATING

*Homespun Essays
from Beech Tree Lane*

DIANNE POSTON OWENS

Praise for *CULTIVATING*

"A wise book that guides the reader into cultivating patience, wonder and hope. The perfect read for those of us struggling to make sense of the world today, which is all of us."

—Susan Breen, Author of *The Fiction Class*

"*Cultivating: Homespun Essays from Beech Tree Lane* is a fascinating, inspiring and refreshing exploration of the everyday that we too often take for granted. Written to the planters, tenders, students and teachers of her own life, skilled journalist Dianne Poston Owens takes us on a journey through what it's like to cultivate our memories and reflections so we may learn "to live a more thoughtful if not restful and peaceful life." If you follow Owens' lead through her many effortless essays filled with wisdom and optimism (especially in times of deep change), you will come to know that the best things happen when we cultivate them."

—Stephanie Austin Edwards,
Author of *What We Set in Motion: A Novel*

"*Cultivating* is a charming and insightful collection of essays, poems, and photography that is truly a gift of Dianne's experiences and her perceptive eye. Written during chaotic times, it has the effect of calming, forcing introspection, and reflection. We learn through her words to appreciate the joys of nature and the beauty of our world, and our past."

—Georgia Griebel Gates,
Author of the Baker Street Bistro Mystery series

"Rich with imagery and life lessons, *Cultivating* is a collection of stories that welcomes you to sit a while under the shade of your favorite tree and ponder days gone by, and how you'll gather yourself for the ones ahead. Clear your calendar for the day and spend a little time reflecting. You won't regret it!"

—Gina Heron, Author of The Pearl Girls series

"Most people long for the opportunity to return to the simpler life of their childhood, or better yet, to the time of their grandparents. In *Cultivating*, author Dianne Owens weaves memories and current events to guide the reader to a place of peace within the chaos. Poignant and impactful."

—Regina Smeltzer,
Author of *Deadly Decision* and
other suspenseful Christian novels

Cultivating is dedicated
to the family members who came before me
and to those who will come along after I'm gone.
To the planters and tenders, to the students and teachers
in the family I know and the one I've yet to meet,
I dedicate this collection of essays.
"Forever is composed of nows," Emily Dickinson said.

Introduction

Hi there! Thank you for picking up a copy of *Cultivating: Homespun Essays from Beech Tree Lane.* If you read my first book of essays, *Gathering*, you know the kind of adventure you're about to take. If not, no worries. You will soon be lost in memories and reflections of your own as you read through a few of mine.

I come from a long line of journal keepers, and cultivators. They were farmers, teachers, writers, and homesteaders. *Thinkers.* They had to be. How can you make a living off the land without putting thought into it? The best things happen because we cultivate them. Give them a little mindfulness, a little nurturing, a little push, a little pull. Juicy ripe red tomatoes will not grow if you buy and plant yellow tomato seeds. Ripe, juicy red tomatoes will not grow in your garden if you don't buy, then plant, the seeds from the purchased packet. If the seeds receive no water, there will be no juicy tomatoes. It is true some things burst forth seemingly of their own accord, but those things are the products of unseen cultivators.

I am a slow-life chronicler, a curator of what I see and do, an observer trying to make sense of the usual and the routine. I live on family land that was once a farm. Today we cultivate bees and trees with shade and a quiet life.

Tomorrow we will likely cultivate a different crop. I travel a little, take photographs of what tickles my imagination, and then I share those captured moments. I was once a journalist, a reporter of life around me. I believe technology has made us all reporters of some sort now.

I put this book together during turbulent times. There is/was a virus infecting us, a pandemic borne through the air we breathe. There is/was societal unrest, the exaggerating and understating of fears and encounters and their causes and meanings. There is/was work to be done in finding solutions to the unrest. There is/was the economy swooning over its lovers (goods and services), languishing because we had no need of the unnecessary. What is/was cultivated during this time is yet to be yielded, harvested.

Amidst this backdrop, I welcome you to my world of essays, musings, philosophizing, photos, thoughts, and ponderings. Use these pictures and words for encouragement, inspiration, reflection, and remembering on the way to living a more thoughtful, if not restful and peaceful, life.

xoxoxo,
Dianne

Essays (Table of Contents)

Photos (Table of Contents)

Hello Again from Beech Tree Lane

It's a nondescript half-mile one-lane dirt drive, this Beech Tree Lane. At its end, if you make it that far, because the lost often turn around before then, the lane devolves into a path into the woods where the beech trees have landed. That's the real end of the road.

This sheltered, oft-hidden path leads to the slough that leads to the Lynches River and its black water. In days gone by the river was the road to the land. Houses built in early America faced the rivers. Those were the highways.

My beeches gather with the pines, oaks, and river birches and are good neighbors to the cypresses. The beeches navigate the seasons and traverse the years. They are not the oldest trees in the woods, but they persevere, replicate and are among the tallest. They bloom in spring, give shade in summer, offer fruit in fall, and give copper penny leaves on which to walk in winter. One doesn't cultivate beech trees. They cultivate themselves.

Beech Tree Lane leads you to the front porch of my house, where most days folks are welcome. They visit, sit a spell, and rock in chairs designed to carry away tears and fears. Some days I rock alone. No intruders.

Today, I invite you onto my porch. From here, we will

discuss what you're cultivating, what nature shows us about planning and creating, and a little about expectations and disappointments.

Let's sit a spell and see where our rocking takes us.

The house at sunset in summer, Beech Tree Lane

Raising a Good Crop

We are cultivators, a people born to cultivate, create and perpetuate. We take the seeds of plants and animals, relationships and ideas, thoughts and visions, and we massage them into the soil, into the linings of uteruses, into our hearts and minds.

We pursue birth, the creation of new. We care and knead and tend.

I once cross-stitched a saying onto a piece of fabric. It kept me a little saner for a while. By this, I mean it helped ease my mind. It reminded me that I was cultivating as best I could, doing my part in the process. This phrase stitched on fabric gave me hope that I was doing okay. My work was satisfactory. It, and thus I, was acceptable. I (we) need to know that, that when we're cultivating, I'm (we're) doing okay, all right. Okay and all right are simple, little words. They have a bigger meaning, that all is as it should be and is enough.

The unknown results of our cultivations may make cultivating iffy. We may want to abandon the cultivating, as it takes our time, effort, money, and mental attention and challenges us as we use our resources and resourcefulness. We may attempt or appear to abandon the cultivating while, in reality, we have only pushed it off.

"Do what you can, where you are, with what you have."

Crucial words from a noted overachiever who was likely seeking balance within perfection. The words give permission to create, cultivate, to exist without being frantic about where you are, what you have or don't have. The framed fabric and stitched words have been lost, but the phrase is ever with me.

When I cross-stitched those words onto cloth for a wall-hanging, I was learning, and I am still learning (because truths do not change), that there is always more to do than can be done. And doing my best is not always going to accomplish what I want my best to accomplish.

The best-laid plans go awry. Far awry. I can cultivate. I cannot control what follows. I may plant, create, nurture, and tend, but the results of my efforts are left to the variables and elements I do not control. Results come after they are exposed to time and temperatures, to rain, wind, sunshine, and thorns. More times than not, I have been unaware or been wrong about the thorns and their locations.

It is difficult to live a perfect life—no burnt toast, no bad meals, a clean house, perfect cookies for every bake sale, purchasing clothes that don't go out of style for the body at a perfect weight and body mass index, perfectly well-coifed hair, meeting every deadline and exceeding all expectations.

It is nearly impossible to never run out of gas (me personally or my vehicle) and not to have a vehicle that needs maintenance. Things and people must be maintained. Perfect health. Terrific teeth. Successful and sexy spouse. Always. Just. So. But we try.

Trying to pursue perfection has taught me that not

only is it difficult to be perfect and live a perfect life, it is impossible—elusive.

What is perfect for one is not perfect for another. What was perfect then is not perfect now. Cultivating is doing what you can, where you are, with what you have and leaving the results with other cultivators, and, in the end, with the Great Cultivator. And that is in itself a form of perfection. I do the best I can, given the information I have, in the circumstances at the time, with whatever I have at hand. If it is not perfect, it is enough, because it is all I have.

We cultivate land by plowing the soil, sowing seeds, and tending what grows. If we are blessed to enjoy some measure of luck, we get to harvest useful crops. And while I can put a seed in the ground, I cannot control where its roots grow, and if the seed germinates. As a seed gives way to becoming a plant, I also have to cultivate weed control.

I can cultivate a new language or friendship or skill as I cultivate improvement in my time management skills and seek to cultivate better work habits. I can cultivate good manners and civility and kindness. Or I can cultivate their opposites: loneliness, boredom, laziness, and their other friends, discontent and malevolence.

Our arms may feel like wet noodles, our knees may ache from use. Our feet may throb from effort. And yet we cultivate. It is what we do, and what we don't do.

What are you unconsciously cultivating?

Where might you cultivate?

Beech Tree roots
They cling, they endure.
Roots run, restless in the earth.
Greenville, South Carolina

Patient Mother Nature

Nature is a patient teacher. Mother Earth silently lectures us on the virtues of perseverance each time what we call a weed pushes up from the dirt between the cracks on the sidewalk, seemingly destined to be trampled by foot traffic.

Pushing forward, up, is always worth it. Sometimes the plant is allowed to reach maturity unencumbered by what is going on around it. I once wrote a story about a collard plant which grew in the space between the sidewalk and the feed, seed and hardware store.

Fully grown, it was green and lush with yellow flowers. It made a pretty picture in the weekly hometown newspaper. The collard that could. And did. Perseverance, patience, production.

Sometimes, these plants found in the cracks bloom for a season. Sometimes they are picked and lovingly placed into vases with other weeds. They take us to school. We can thrive in the cracks.

What was the last lecture you heard from something you saw in nature?

Where is your favorite spot from which to observe nature?

Dandelion in the Acline Street sidewalk
Lake City, South Carolina

Pandemic Cleansing

This year, 2020, people living in Punjab, India, saw views of the Himalayas clearly from their homes for the first time in years. Some say the peaks have not been seen in twenty-five to thirty years, leaving many to have lived their entire lives not knowing they had a magnificent view of the mountains.

Their views have been obstructed by pollution. Like millions around the world, the people responded to the call to stay home. There is/was a pandemic, a new contagious disease among us, spreading exponentially. Something that steals air from lungs. Maybe the cats are getting it, too.

Cars, buses, planes, trains, motorcycles all stayed home, too. There has been, simply put, less pollution in the air. Because people stayed home to stay healthy, the air grew healthier and the views became unforgettable.

Here in South Carolina, our April and May were the most gorgeous in years. Breathable air, not heavily laden with humidity. It was nice not to breathe water. Was it, too, because we humans managed to affect the weather for the good? We won't know. April was just being April, and May was May.

The flowers were showy. Prouder than ever to be themselves. Because they had an audience? There they were— the roses, the iris, the petunias, the mums returned from

September. The gladiolas, azaleas, magnolia blooms, and gardenias. Peering down, looking out, doing what they do, being what they are.

There is much that goes on around us that we do not see, cannot know, will not admit is there. The gift of a pandemic, for some, has been clarity.

I fret for those who cannot feel what cleaner air can do. I pray for those who willingly are exposed. I mourn those who paid the price so I would be told to stay home. I stayed close to home. Not always inside it, however. Tough thing, obedience.

I will remember the daylilies and daisies. My amaryllis.

How did the novel virus named COVID-19 change you and your world?

What was made clearer to you during your most recent pandemic?

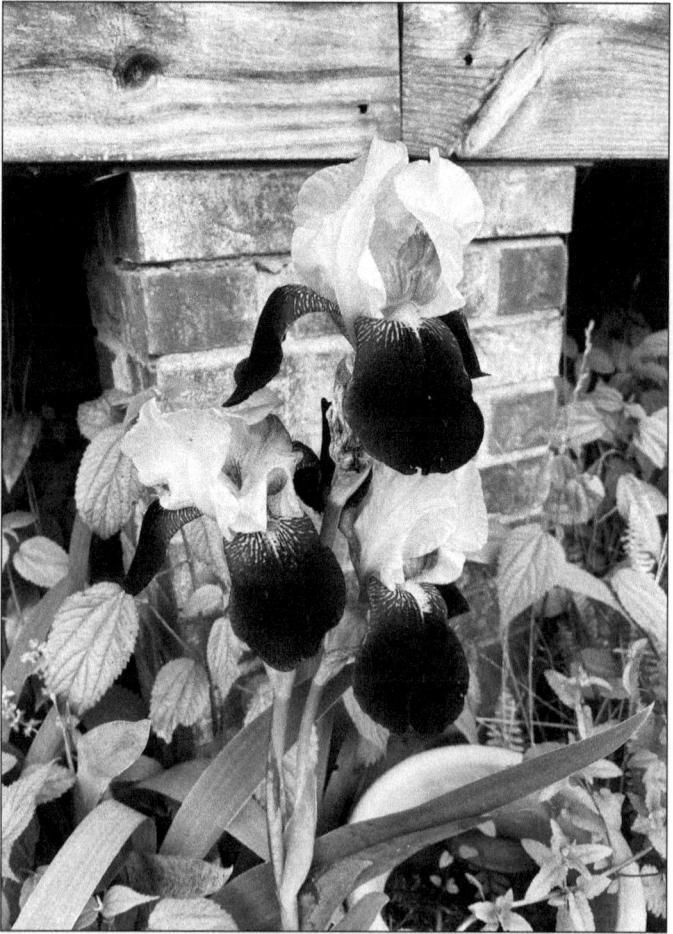

Purple and white
bearded iris in 2020,
during the late, great malady

Hearing the Humming

While I intellectually knew a hummingbird was called a "humming" bird because of the sound its wings make when it flits about, I was more than fifty years old before I sat still long enough, in the right place, to hear their sounds for myself.

I was perched in the porch hammock swing when the whirring commanded my attention. I was befuddled by the noise and could not for the life of me discover where it was coming from. Putting down the book in my hands, I concentrated hard, scanning the area. Was my cell phone chirping?

I thought perhaps it was the sound of a dozen flies. A big horsefly? It was a mild spring day. Picture perfect. To my right were the hummingbird feeders. There it was again. The whirring, and then a chittering. A faraway drone?

No, it was not a nuisance horsefly or a snooping neighbor. It was the whirring and chittering of a thrilling new song. New to me, that is. This was not new to Mr. Ruby-Throated.

Never had I heard the humming of the tiny bird's wings. I had no frame of reference. Never had I heard the distinctive way they talk among themselves. I had admired them through windows, me on the inside looking out, but I had never sat still long enough, close enough, to know the sounds of a hummingbird.

A hummingbird simply goes about doing what it does, whirring among its friends, chittering away. The sound is breathless, busy-ness incarnate. To me it was nothing short of miraculous. The whirring is the sound of a thousand tiny horses' hooves on a sandy beach, the wind through the beech tree leaves in fall, the sound of dirt flinging itself into the air when a baseball player slides into home plate in time to claim the run.

The sound is all energy, urgency, and need. Before the hearing of the wings and songs, hummingbirds were to me time travelers who graced me each spring and summer without fail, just magically appearing. And then disappearing. They dictated my plantings, the lantana is for them, and I fed them. I thought I could only watch them through glass.

Now I know, though. I know their sounds and I am invited, as a special friend, to listen to their conversations. I take every opportunity to sit close enough to see them, hear what they have to say to me and to anyone who will be still and listen. If, in fact, cultivating is a process and nature is a patient and diligent teacher, I had been a bored and complacent student.

Where do you sit to learn from what is in the natural world around you?

What surprise from nature do you share with others?

Hummingbird in Hannah

Making the Most of It

I try to start as many days as I can before sunrise so I can be there when *"it"* happens.

"It" is the moment when the coolness of the night that was slips away from the earth and into the air and all that is natural and real understands, without knowing why, that the night is gone and day has come.

"It" lasts only about as long as a firefly's light. And if you're not looking, you won't see *"it."* The sun breaks over and through and around and begins conducting the events of a new day.

The sky catches the sun and lets it paint with its embers. Even if there is fog or rain or wind, *"it"* happens. *"It"* always is.

"It" is the starting anew of the day. *"It"* is an every-day gift.

"Forget the former things; don't dwell on the past. See, I am doing a new thing! Now it springs up; do you not perceive it?" (Isaiah 43: 18-19).

"The beginning is always today," Mary Wollstonecraft Shelley said.

Where holds the **"it"** *wonder for you?*

What is **"its"** *importance?*

Waterfall en route to Pumpkintown, South Carolina
Where it comes from, no one knows, but on and on it goes.
One way or another, whether I'm here, or not.
The running water over rocks offering refreshment, rest.
It is.

For the Love of Aprons

I am an avid fan of aprons. You know those things that cover your clothes when you're in a kitchen? Or perhaps when painting? I hope they make a comeback.

First, I sort of grew up when aprons were commonplace. No remarks about age are due. Aprons were a way of life in the kitchen to protect clothes from stains. And they were worn when cooking indoors or out. They had pockets or not. But, oh, they were so much more than just a protective covering for clothes.

Second, I reenact history. In that period of time, the eighteenth century, the year is specifically 1780 for me, aprons were a mainstay of a woman's dress. Again, primarily for protecting the fancier clothes, but again, aprons performed many more useful functions.

Not too long ago, I received an e-mail, complete with photos of a pattern from which to create, or sew, *"the apron."* Someone along the e-mail trail of people who had forwarded this to whomever sent it to me said, "Mom and her apron were like Siamese twins." What a picture! A cook would not have been seen without her apron. Inseparable. Attached.

I have passed to my daughters the aprons their grandmothers and great-grandmothers wore. But more, I'd like to see all cooks use them once again. The e-mail read (and I've paraphrased along the way) something like this:

The pattern size for the apron is *"medium,"* defined as a size 14-16. (How's that for refreshing!) The principal use of the apron is to protect the dress underneath because moms and grandmas have so few. Making a fresh apron is easier than making new clothes and uses less material.

Aprons serve as potholders for moving hot pans from the stove and oven to the table. (This is even true of items moved from a microwave!)

Aprons are wonderful for drying tears and sopping up messes. (They also collect tears and spills as a depository for things that need to be discarded.)

From the chicken coop or garden, from the pear, apple or fig tree, the apron can be used to carry anything that needs toting after being fetched.

If company comes a callin', shy three-year-olds can easily hide their faces and be sheltered from strangers. A swipe with the apron will undust most readily-viewed tabletops.

If a cool breeze blows up unexpectedly, arms may be wrapped into aprons for warmth. Aprons may be used to wipe the sweat off your brows (especially when cooking over a hot wood-fired stove or the backyard gas grill).

The email closed with, "They would go crazy now trying to figure out how many germs were on that apron. I don't think I ever caught anything from an apron but love . . ."

And then one day near Christmas, at the Johnsonville (South Carolina) Artisan Outpost on Marion Street, I met a woman who sewed aprons. There they were, for sale, making a comeback.

I am an avid fan of aprons.

What catches your tears and spills?

What besides aprons needs to make a comeback in today's world?

Homemade aprons for sale at a crafters market.
Grandmama Lee carried a petite folded knife
in her pocket, along with a hankie.
Mainstays of the old ways.

Spider Lilies Have Secrets, Too

I look for them every year and they never disappoint. I love spotting the first jonquil in spring. Around home, if the weather is just right, that's usually February. Then, each fall, I thrill at the discovery of the first spider lily. I start looking for them in mid-September.

Spider lilies have that one thin, tall stalk with a willowy, lacy, spindly flower at the top. The flowers can be white, red, or a variation between. They are all around us all the time. In the earth, we just can't see them. Until, poof! There they are at the edge of the field, in a lot where a house once lived, or a flower bed. The bulbs seem to me to thrive in cemeteries and on forgotten lands.

They burst forth after a good rain, brightening a dismal day, heralding fall and winter. And then they slowly disappear, back, as it is, into the earth until next year.

I have a writer friend who recently wrote about mushrooms in her online blog. She said, "It rained for five days here in Darlington . . . finally, the sun came out, and along with the sun, a myriad of mushrooms." She said she closely examined them, hoping some were edible. Alas, hers were not. They were the poisonous ones.

Still, they were intricately designed and quite pretty.

"Some are fluted, while others looked like the homes

of Smurfs," she wrote. She asked, "Where have they been all this time?" Then she did her research. "My mushrooms have been there all along, underground, eating off the dead vegetation and decomposing roots hidden beneath the grass. When a good rain comes, they develop 'fruiting structures' which show above ground."

Like my spider lilies or jonquils, *my dandy lions* or amaryllis, mushrooms are there, just waiting to happen, cultivated only by time, temperature and the ground they lie within. They exist under the surface, and then poof! Magic! They spring to life. Their secret is within them, within the soil, within their roots, all just out of sight, under the ground.

Regina drew a parallel between the mushrooms and humanity. "For a time, we can keep the nasty parts of our lives hidden—habits we don't like to admit or thoughts that don't show on the surface. But eventually, the rain will come in the form of temptation, stress, or anger, and POP, out it comes, that fruiting structure no one knew was in us." I'll let you contemplate that for yourself.

Me? I like to know things can come from unprepared soil. That life springs forth when and where we least expect it and with no effort on our parts. Living things survive in the tiniest bit of dirt between the cracks of a busy sidewalk, in pedestrian's unintended garden.

The secret is underground.

Cultivating

When was the last time you planted something just to watch it grow?

What has sprung up, into your life that caught you by surprise?

September's Spider Lilies
Surviving, surprising,
Delightfully alive.
Soldiers of their soil.

Work with the Wind

My brothers and I spent many Thanksgivings raking leaves. There were four of us, and looking back at it, I see what the grandparents saw – arms and legs to help with a chore.

At the time, I thought it was a torturous ritual, a ridiculous way to spend a national holiday. I also knew there was no getting out of it. Now, I see us in the back yard working hard, having a little fun, being silly while learning a lesson and helping the g'parents, God rest their souls. My brothers' memories, as is often the case, are different from mine. I'll let them have their memories and any lessons they learned. Tough work, we were in it together and somehow that made it tolerable, if not all right, with me.

Note to self: What is tough now may become a wonderful memory, smiled upon later, sort of a *"that which doesn't kill us makes us stronger"* kind of thing. Embrace it. You never know.

Through raking at my grandparents, I learned the merits of doing something for others without getting paid. Granted, the meal we received was a wondrous one, but the payment was in doing the job so our grandparents wouldn't have to do it. Self-satisfaction, without the smugness often attributed to it. Satisfaction because we had contributed, cleaned a yard, helped out.

Working with my brothers, I learned the power of teamwork. You start on one side of the yard, and with three others, you cut your work time into fourths and get to the other side of the yard at four times the pace you would set by yourself. Surround yourself with a good team.

I learned the yard looks better if you rake it. Maintaining what you have is time well spent.

I learned satisfaction comes from a job well done, brought in under budget and on time.

I learned to obey the leader in a situation. They are the leaders. Keeping rules is usually necessary for a civilized society to function. Questioning the rules is an acceptable part of a functioning team.

Make sure you have a leader worth following, and ask the right questions.

I learned that though my brothers and I raked together, and we share that same experience, we were at different ages and stages in our lives. What we learned through raking and how we remember those experiences is an individual venture. At the heart of an experience, each gets from it what is necessary for them. We can be in the same place, at the same time, doing the same thing, but we will relive it and remember it differently. That's okay. We were, and are, each at different ages and heights. We will see things differently.

Those raking days showed me that this grandfather was one of the bravest, strongest, smartest men on earth. His bravery was barely mentioned, but we knew he was a survivor of World War II and had seen places I only knew about from a globe. He was also a mean drunk and a fighter.

He could stand under and lift the swing set with his bare hands. He won every arm-wrestling contest in which I saw him compete. And he taught us how to properly rake.

It takes a smart man to know about proper raking.

"It's good to work hard. It's better to rake with the wind."

Why fight it? We need all the help we can get.

In what ways are you raking into the wind?

What rule do you live by that comes from nature?

Roy.
Another raking with the wind
one summer day in June.

Hope

Honestly,
opinion doesn't matter.
Opinions wing away with the seasons,
nectar for the foolish.
The Promise
has been made, prospect of
Eternity.
It is so.
There is hope.
Do not let your heart
be troubled.
A place is prepared for us.
We will be where we are to be.
Have we need
of anything more? There is
an Offer more than we can
Plan. Or understand.
Eternity.

Some trees have faces
In the woods in South Carolina

She Said We Are Becoming

We are all on the way to becoming more, better, new, different. That's what Gwendolyn says during many of our discussions at the book club in the library. She does not want to be the same yesterday as she was the day before. In that, she is consistent.

The "me" you see when you meet me is a new me, because every day is a new day. The same is true for you. Or it should be. You are what you have read, seen, felt, experienced, tossed aside, and kept.

My mom once told my older brother, her first born, that she didn't know what to do with a sixteen-year-old son. She'd never had one before. Along with that, she'd never been whatever age it was she was then, either.

They were both doing the best they could, with what they had, right where they were. Every day is surely a new day. We count on it. We hope in it.

When we meet someone, what we see before us is the one who has withstood, become jaded, endured the crushing of dreams, and felt pain. Or, just maybe, we are introduced to the victorious one, the champion, the one healed.

We meet people. They meet us. We do well to remember we, us, we are all in our *"becoming."* No one has arrived.

Sometimes we see what we want to see. At least twice

now I have seen things that weren't there. I once convinced myself there was a dead squirrel dangling from a utility line that stretched across Killian Road. Every day I drove under that line and saw this fried-looking remnant and felt sorry for the apparently electrocuted critter.

I pointed it out to others in the car with me. For weeks we stared up. Discussed it. Until one day...

One day, for whatever reason, traffic was slower than usual and we were stopped under the dead squirrel. Only it wasn't a dead squirrel hanging onto a utility line. It was just the remains of a small tree limb. Things were not as they appeared at a glance, when going by at forty-five miles an hour.

Another time, I stepped off the back stoop to walk out into the grass on a warm spring morning. I saw a snake. It raised its ugly head and shook it at me. I threw my apple at it to chase it away. It did not flee but shook and shook its little brown, pointed head at me.

I threw a few more things at my snake to chase it away, before I came to understand it was not going to wiggle away. It would not flee because it wasn't scared of me. It would not flee because it was a leaf that would just keep looking at me until it disintegrated.

I felt sorry for the dead squirrel, electrocuted before its time. I feared meeting the wiggly snake. In the end, I was misled by my interpretation of what I saw, based on what I have seen before and likely expected to see.

I remember this truth when I meet someone. They may not be what I expect them to be. I cannot judge their book, their story, by its cover. I sure hope they know the same about me and give me the benefit of the doubt.

I am, we all are, on the way to becoming more, better, new, different. Hope returns, the one bemoaning life in the Book of Lamentations says, when they remember this one thing: unfailing love and mercy continue, fresh each morning, sure as the sunrise.

Be patient with me. I am not all you see. Every day is a new day.

When did you last make a discovery that was different from what you first assumed?

What is a preconceived notion about people that you carry with you?

Divinely delight in the moment
A Florida vacation

Pardon You

In from the cold
Searching,
seeking
shelter.
Hoping,
happiness
to find
to mend
the brokenhearted
To forgive
the unkind.

Once upon a winter in South Carolina

The Uncovering

The earth has secrets. I have questions. Who was here before me? Where did they come from? Seekers, historians, and archeologists search out answers to these questions.

They dig in the earth, in books containing research, in museums with collections put together by others who have dug before.

We can guess at what the finds from the diggings mean. We sift and brush and sift again.

We come close to understanding what we find when we dig. But the earth has its secrets and it won't share.

I am not good at the tedious work of uncovering a find. Thankfully, there are those who are. Patience.

I don't like waiting. Get to it! Now! The earth yields more answers to the patient ones.

Arrowheads, potsherds, coins, buttons and pipes are turned up by water, wind, time, tiny shovels and small brushes.

There is the keeping, the cataloguing. Brown paper bags. Excitement in the tedium. It is not enough to make a find—the found thing has to be taken in context. What else is there with it?

Biologists and botanists are called in for conversations

about pollen content. Collaboration brings information. Cooperation adds understanding.

Look along the river, and in the roots of the upended tree. Who was here before me?

Where did they go? All living things have mysteries.

Where did the dry creek run? When did the oxbow lake form?

Where are the bones?

Dig deep. Brush carefully. Don't overlook.

The earth has her secrets. Only some she shares.

What secrets do you keep covered?

What secrets have you uncovered?

An alleyway wall in Marion, South Carolina

Beech Trees in Summer

The feet of elephants. That's what the base of the American beech tree shows above the earth. Below the earth are arms twisted with grabbing and holding and caring. Grey, thick, strong feet. Grey, thick, strong arms.

Beech trees in spring and summer spread their roots, spread their crowns and yawn. They are tall, strong, and usually live three to four hundred years. Fagus grandifolia, the American beech, is the only member of the genus native to North America. They grow in groves, as they seek to replicate themselves.

Some research sources suggest that ancient runes, the earliest of books, were written on beech wood tablets or slabs. You can leave your mark on a beech tree. I know beech trees hold their summer stories for the next generation to read.

From beech wood comes furniture (giving us places on which to rest), railroad ties (helping us get to where we want to be), and parquet flooring (shoring us up from below).

Beech trees make good homes. Their nut is edible by those living in the branches and being sheltered under the limbs.

The beech trees with which I am most familiar and

embrace as family are grounded in the ooze along the Lynches River in South Carolina. And though I've not seen traces here among my beeches, yet, those in other states are facing blight. First came a bark-infesting fungus that worked to bring the trees to their knees.

Now, something new that doesn't love the beech tree is killing it. Killing the leaves, which in turn choke out the tree. Small ones can die within three years. They are not allowed to become well- rooted.   The microbe killer, perhaps a leaf-eating critter too tiny to see, has been described as an "invasive alien pest."

An unseen, infectious, communicable disease is spreading among my beloved beech trees. As their leaves die, the canopy of shade provided to the dirt beneath the tree diminishes. Light gets in. The soil shoots forth things resting, things that do not grow in shade. The forest changes.

When beech trees cannot replicate themselves, the world changes. I haven't cultivated beech trees, they cultivated themselves. I am guilty of taking them for granted, of knowing they will be here because they have been here. I expect them to be here.

My expectations are not enough. In time, there may not be any elephant-footed trunks where this tree meets the ground. Natural selection? Only the strong survive? Adapt and change or die? There's a struggling yew in Florida, a vanishing loulu in Hawaii, and the extinct Saint Helena olive.

I do not like pests. I do love beech trees in summer. I

am heartbroken. A harsher winter may come to our beeches and they may leave us.

How many things that used to be native to where you live are now gone?

What do you know about the dodo bird?

Elephant-Footed Beech Tree

I Stand Corrected

I remember my dad spanking me only once. That one spanking lasted me a long time. I'm sure I probably needed and received many more spankings. Oops! Now let's stop right there and review that sentence. What I needed and received was correction. The prescribed method of the day was not spoiling the child by not sparing the rod. I was not abused.

There's a proverb that says that the rod and reproof give wisdom. Sometimes one will do, sometimes the other, and sometimes both are required. "Children, left to themselves," the proverb says, "bring shame to their mothers. Correct your children and they give you rest. They will give your soul delight." These words certainly have been misused by some, for sure. Thankfully, that was never my case.

Usually such administrations of discipline, grounding or otherwise, were administered by my mom. I'm not mad at her for it. She was usually the one who recognized that I was in need of correction. She taught me to behave. After that one time with my dad, I got smart. I learned to behave for him, too.

I quickly learned not to stand between him and the TV, and not to mock him about said standing. I was at that smart-alecky age of seven-ish to eight-ish. I bounced into the main room of the house and bravely stood between my dad, who was reclining on the couch, and the television and its black-and-white version of the show he was intently watching.

Did I want his attention? Nope. I was just being silly and mean. I knew what I was doing. I taunted him. I brazenly stood there and stared at him. I defied him to do anything about my stance.

Probably because I knew my dad was a patient person.

Picture my hands on my hips, making myself as large as possible so he couldn't see the TV.

"Move," he suggested.

I didn't take the hint. I thought, "What a great game!"

"Mov-ah," he said a little louder, because he knew if I hadn't moved, I must not have heard him.

I well remember doing a little confident hip-moving sassy dance at this point, trying to cover as much of the screen behind me as possible. Dum-de-dum-dum.

"MOV-AH!"

And then I pushed it too far.

"Mov-ah me yourselfah," I suggested.

So, he did.

I know I never stood between my dad and that television ever again. I came to respect his right to watch unobstructed television. Without question.

It only took a second for me to realize this had not been "the time nor the place" for me to pick and tease, which we'll talk about later. I've often wondered why this moment made such an impact on me and why I remember it as if it was yesterday.

But I know the answer. I knew the answer that day. He showed me how easily he could move me, and how easily I could disappoint him, and how silly it was to be deliberately mean to someone. I should have had more respect for my dad, who at one time worked three jobs to keep the family of six in the middle of the classes.

My excuse is that I was young. I was learning appropriate and inappropriate behavior.

He was a tolerant man who usually laughed away my antics. I knew he was right. I knew I should have moved. I should have kissed him on the cheek and either joined him in watching TV or left the room. I had choices. I chose to mock and defy.

I chose poorly.

It's a lesson I never forgot. I can still hear my voice in my head when I'm made to do something I don't want to do: "Mov-ah me yourself-ah."

Sometimes, I am that same child, the one who behaves poorly, who needs correction.

Was there a time you got away with doing something you knew was wrong?

Why does correction give wisdom?

Maximillian

Where Dolphins Play

There was a shy murmur
tender to the ear
breathing hushed,
vanquishing fear.

I leaned and listened,
feeling salted tears.

There is a place
where the dolphins play
where the sea and sky meet day after day.

I was allowed there once,
then swept away.
Could I but seize the gift to return,
then stay!

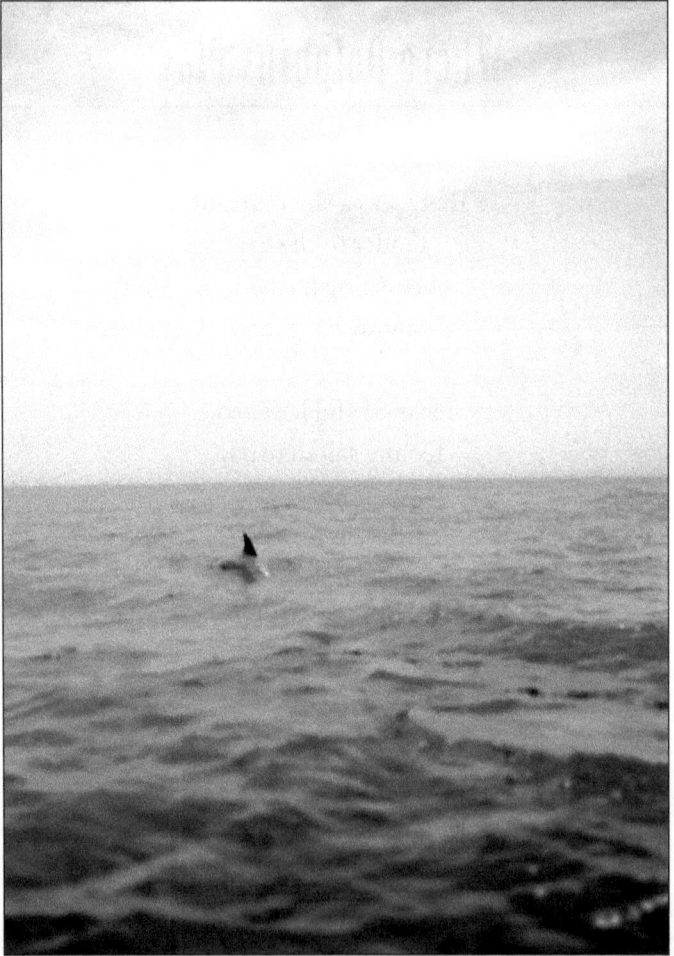

Out and about near Jacksonville, Florida

Tips for Life

Your Household Guide, 1951: "Before working in the garden, or doing other rough work, rub your fingernails over a piece of soap. This will prevent the earth from getting in under the nails, and when you wash your hands the soap comes out easily."

I tried it. Gloves work best. Perhaps soap under the nails and gloves work best of all. Soft soap doesn't work at all. Just wanted you to know.

"To keep crisp cookies crisp, and soft cookies soft, place only one kind in a cookie jar." I suppose the moral here is some things just ought not be stored together. After all, cookies will be affected by their surroundings.

And, I kid you not, right on page 42: "Spinach may be the broom of the stomach, but sauerkraut is the vacuum cleaner." I have nothing to say to that. Well, of course I do, but I am exercising your right not to hear it or read it!

I received as a gift what I believe is a small silver overnight case. Inside are 1960-70s era recipes clipped from newspapers and magazines. From desserts to dinners, the typed instructions are often accompanied by hand-written notes.

"Stir more here." The arrow points to the butter and

shortening, just before adding the sugar, and is written on the December 25, 1961, recipe for chocolate pound cake.

"Try this," is written on the *Farm Journal Square Doughnuts* recipe. I wonder if the baker in the family ever tried them, or were they left to be baked another day? I'll give you the glaze recipe:

> Blend 2 cups sifted confectioners' sugar,
> 1/3 cup milk, and 1 teaspoon vanilla.
> Dip the warm doughnuts in the glaze.
> Drain on a rack over waxed paper.

You can reuse your glaze drippings, the food editor said.

Recipes provide tips for cooking, baking, stewing, and roasting. Some of us create concoctions and call them casseroles. Some of us follow recipes. Some of us may even reuse the drippings.

What "tips" do you pass on to others?

Where do you get your recipes for living?

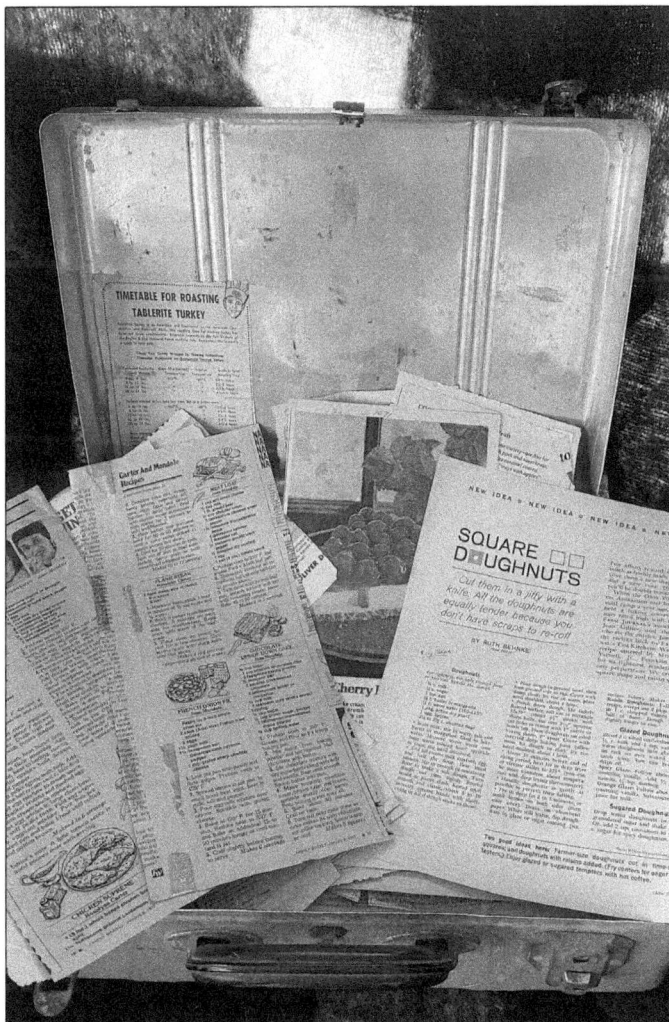

Collection of Tips

On the Occasion of the 41st Anniversary of My 21st Birthday

I was born in the early afternoon on a hot summer day, in the United States' South, sixty miles inland from the Atlantic Ocean. I left the state, traveled a bit, and then I spent a few years trying to "get back home."

I'm here now, home, living on a hill overlooking a swamp on the edge of a small river which feeds into a larger river that empties into the ocean. I am, for all practical purposes, all about the water.

After all, it was inevitable. Observe these facts regarding my life:

I was born on a Monday. Monday is the day of the week named for the moon.

I was born under the sign of cancer, the crab, often called the moon child. The moon rules the waters' waves, creating the ebb and flow of high and low tides. Crabs get their existence from the water.

And summer days in my South mean heat. Stinky, sweaty heat and humidity. Humidity is, after all, the amount of water in the air. And then, most of those hot summer days end in a thunder shower.

I won't continue to go into detail here, but suffice it to

say that this ebb, flow, crabbiness and storminess may be indicative of moodiness and to my being given to bouts of melancholy. I am loud when I laugh, which is often. Not unlike a crashing wave on a beach. I don't get depressed, though melancholy can look like depression to others.

Consider the crab: I'm a little introverted. Specifically, think fiddler crab, with its wisp of a shell, burying into the sand. I am terribly extroverted when around friends who can handle me being me, i.e., picture here fiddler crabs all racing to the water, loving to make a full-hearted splash.

I remember turning twenty-one years old. It was that long-sought-for birthday, that one that marked the beginning of the rest of my life. At least in recent history, twenty-one was advertised as the absolute end of childhood, adolescence, and anything less than adulthood.

It marked the beginning of taking charge and being your own boss. Turning twenty-one was a wonderful event. Mine was spent, where else but at the beach along the Atlantic with friends. To date, I have celebrated many anniversaries of my "twenty-one-ish-ness." I have now celebrated the forty-first anniversary of being twenty-one. And yet again I am at the water's edge. With the passing of this birthday, I find I am a little crabby and moody.

By fourteen I knew I wanted to be a writer and photographer. I wanted to travel and tell stories. I began to work toward that dream. My twenties and thirties were spent learning what independence could be, with travel and new relationships.

My thirties and forties were lumped together and

defined by the pursuits of raising children and earning money and were, therefore, more "otherly directed" than my previous years. My fifties and sixties have been and are gifts to myself. I continue to celebrate, take beach trips, study the stars, and look to the moon.

And write. And tell stories.

Who do you invest in?

What is the destination of your next trip?

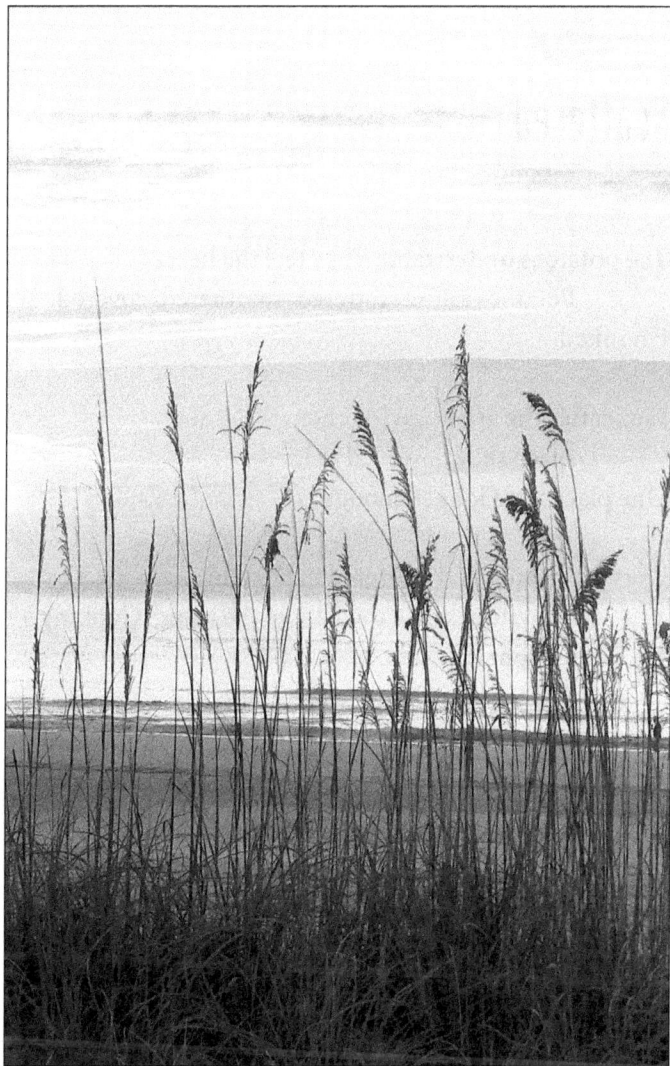

Through the oats and to the sea

Scattered

The potatoes understand. They feel the heat.
> Potatoes know scattered, smothered, covered.
Chunked.

We scatter the ashes, giving them the space,
> space they deserved in life.
One place is no longer enough.

Eggs are heated and scattered in the pan.
> They, too, know the heat of the thing. Cooking.
Becoming done.
> A piece here, more pieces there.

A thought, a wish,
A flit, a fly,
A gnat, a sigh.

Scattering about is hard work.

I call to my pieces and parts
> to leave their lumps and clumps.

I summon my parts to be a whole
> before my scattering begins again.

Up, and then away

Grandma Lee: A Certified Fifties Lady

Every person shall give as able, according to the blessing which has been given to them; out of our abundance we give.

Grandma is with me every Christmas, even though she hasn't been here for more than thirty-five years. When people die they leave holes. Holes in your heart, holes in how you spend your day, holes in your soul. Just holes.

Some holes are small and seemingly heal in a matter of a few years. Some holes begin healing but are ripped open afresh from some memory or conversation, a smell or sound. Other holes are so huge that time can never create enough scar tissue to bring the jaggedy edges together.

My grandma canned vegetables and fruits and worked hard to grow food that fed her family all year long. She worked from the time she arose until her short little round body lay in bed and she slept. She worked. She slept. She went to church. Her handiwork was prolific.

Eight years after her death I was still eating the plum jelly she had put up for us to enjoy. I wrote in a journal that I served the last of Grandma's plum jelly to friends of mine, whom she'd never met, to a great-grandchild she never knew, by a granddaughter who loves her still and intends she not be forgotten.

I worried that eating the last of the jelly would make her go further away.

I made a pumpkin pie. Not just an ordinary pumpkin pie, but one constructed from following her instructions on a recipe card she gave me the summer before she went to visit her cousin and returned home in body only.

Tonight, the red and green quilt she meticulously stitched together by machine and by hand drapes over me to warm me while I sleep. I can curl up under it and into it and pretend she's with me. She didn't hold me much, but when she did it mattered. She was there. She gave good hugs and received them well.

My chin rested on her head when I was grown. I don't forget that touch of resting there. Her hair was thinned. Sometimes I curled it for her on Saturdays after she washed it in preparation for Sundays, which were always meant for church. Dippity Do.

Most often in the background, she was there from the beginning of my memories.

The quilting frame hung from her kitchen's ceiling. Night after night. Day after day. Stitching. Her fingers ached. Among quilters, her stitches were the more precise. Many envied her work. She would rub her hands but not complain.

A break from quilting meant baking, cooking, cleaning, or preparing foods for the future. There was a bed, so I know she slept.

She tried to make us each a quilt that winter. She nearly

succeeded. She was a woman who knew to keep her crisp cookies and soft cookies separated.

To date, what gift that you've been given do you treasure the most?

What have you given that others treasure?

A Gift to You of Lee's Peanut Brittle

Combine one cup light Karo syrup,
one cup sugar, two cups peanuts.
Cook on medium to high.
(You may have to adjust the heat as you
go, she suggests in her recipe.)
Stir fast until brown.
Add one teaspoon baking soda and
pour quickly onto greased pan.
Let it set up.
Break apart and give away.

Lee Adele Cox Poston, Christmas 1960
Blurry but remembered

Under the Weather

Under the weather. Under the effects of bad weather. Under the effects of some germs. I am reminded that being sick is no fun.

I missed meetings, endured headaches, went through a box of tissues, drank gallons of hot tea (mixed with lemon and honey, and sometimes vinegar), ate peculiarly hot peppermints by the handful and stayed in bed nearly a whole day and a half. I had no energy, felt as if my head was balanced on a toothpick that didn't want to hold it up and my eye sockets hurt.

It had been building. I knew the cold was going to catch me. I felt it run up my back and jump off my head Thursday straight through to Monday morning.

On Monday, I woke up, gargled with Listerine and then with warm salty water. I went to work, but I knew I was losing the battle. By noon, I was done.

I believe in the power of rest and chicken noodle soup.

A few Tylenol sinus capsules and a Mentholatum rub. An ibuprofen at the four-hour mark. Those and a good book are usually all I need in order to get better. If I can't drink coffee and I can't read a good book, call an ambulance. I'm really sick.

Because I didn't want to pass along the cold from hell,

and because I was in a weakened immune state and didn't want to catch anything worse than the bug to which I was tethered, I opted to do what they say to do in most sickly situations—I stayed put. I kept to myself, spraying disinfectant behind me as I went from bed to bathroom to kitchen to bed and back again.

The rules say to gargle with warm, salty water. Gargling, at worst, moistens a sore and scratchy throat and at best brings temporary relief. Do it often enough, for long enough, and maybe, maybe, eventually, the sore throat is gone.

I'm not sure if the gargling chased the cold away, if it was gargled to death, spit out, or given enough time to evaporate on its own. Perhaps I gargled to get my cold to pack its mucous bags and return from whence it came. Oh, how I gargled.

I believe if the chicken noodle soup is hot and salty enough, it can scald the cold right out of you. When done right, it chases the gunk up out of the throat and out the end of the nose. When putting something warm on the inside of your body doesn't seem to work, well then it's time to chase the cold away with a hot, steamy shower. Attack the cold, or the sinus crud from the outside. And there are nasal drops, too.

From the drinking and gargling and steaming, Mentholat-ing and Lysol-ing, on this occasion, I was a stinky, steamy, smelly mess. A body curled around a book, covered by my quilt in the middle of the bed. By Wednesday, I was on the mend, breathing better and walking past a tissue box without wanting to climb in and throw myself a party. Thursday I was back at work and among the living. I survived.

Unfortunately, getting sick is a symptom of living. Yes, there are cold medicines and antibiotics when the time is right. There is the covering of one's face, the coughing into the elbow, and the washing, and rewashing of hands. But sometimes we get sick—under the weather, to-the-bottom-of-the-boat sick, and we have to ride out the storm.

How can we do a better job of taking care of ourselves?

Who passed on to you the home remedies you use to make yourself feel better when you're sick?

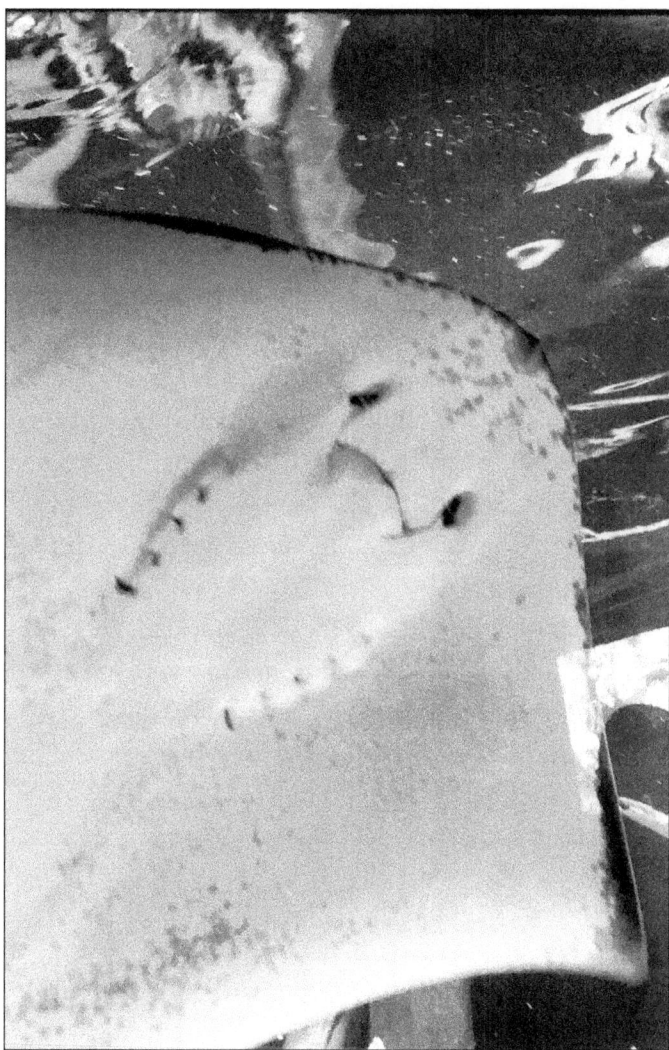

Stanley Stingray, Houston Aquarium

Explorers

What does it mean to fall off the face of the earth?

To go to the edge and disappear? Into nothing. Over and out.

What does it mean to break free from gravity? If that which holds us here is taken away, would we push up and out and away? We would float off the face of the earth?

On the old maps, in the ancient days, there was an end to what could be seen and there were dragons there. A place where all vanish.

Disappear. They had no idea you just keep going, and going, round and round, and round again. If you could, would you come back to where you were? Or are?

Falling off the face of the earth is an impossibility. But some days we'd like to try.

There is gravity. People ought not to say the unkind things.

When was the last time you traveled somewhere you've never been?

Where would you like to go?

Shh. . . I have a secret to tell you.

Liar, Liar, Pants on Fire

I took up running at the age of fifty to prove several points and disprove several others.

Among the lies I'd repeated as truth, believing them in my heart of hearts, were the following:

> My *"over-weightness"* is hereditary and, thus, not my fault.
>
> My eating habits are not the cause of my being overweight.
>
> I have good eating habits.
>
> I have no time to add exercise into my life.
>
> This phase in my life is filled with hormonal issues. I'm not fat, I'm fluffy.
>
> Even if I am obese by the world's doctors' standards, God still loves me.
>
> The fact is, and everyone knows it, counting calories is not nearly as important as counting carbs.
>
> After a certain age a woman simply must accept that she's done all she can do, and it, whatever it is, is just as good as it gets.

Lies! These were some of the lies I told myself. Worse, these were lies I believed.

My grandmothers and other women in my family have weighed more than two hundred pounds. Lovely people, every one. Kind. Generous. Happy. And so was I, too. If Grandmamma Addie said it once she said it a thousand times. I heard her, internalized it, and believed her.

"We may be overweight, but we carry it well."

Along came a young, thin friend who was dissatisfied with many things in her life, not the least of which was a poor cholesterol reading. Good health, it turns out, is everyone's concern—the underweight, the overweight and the just-right weight. Even those who appear *"just right"* are prone to other health issues.

Miss Thin and I, Ms. Biggie, discovered through the blood analysis done at a routine health screening at work that she was, at age thirty, likely headed for a stroke. And that I was obese.

Lies, I tell you. Lies! I wadded up the printed report and threw it in the trash. I was not obese. A little heavy, maybe. But I carried it well.

Oh, the lies we rely on to keep us from doing what we need to do.

And so, we took to running as a way to lower her cholesterol. It became a team thing. I took to running because I used to love it when I was in college and thought the camaraderie we enjoyed while helping her control her cholesterol would be fun.

I am not speedy, but I do love the wind in my hair.

Besides, I wanted to prove that I was right. That exercise would not drastically alter my weight. After all, I am the way the good Lord made me.

We started with a *"Couch to 5K"* walking and running program, and we began charting the foods we ate.

I was to use an online application on my phone to chart my food choices. Easy, I thought, until I realized I wasn't eating two cookies, as the suggested serving said, but eight cookies. And this is the honest truth; though I know I've explained what a liar I am, I lied to the online food chart, looking around to make sure no one was watching me enter erroneous data, and I told it I'd eaten four cookies. The compromise.

I broke out in a sweat. In that moment, when I entered invalid calorie consumption into a smarter-than-me phone app, I realized just how many lies I'd been telling myself.

The light bulb went on right over my head. If I kept lying to myself, I wasn't proving my initial points but rather proving I didn't know what I was talking about—at all!

It took a little time, about ten months total, but I lost forty pounds. I re-learned the value in honestly counting all calories and their nutritional importance.

I learned that you lose weight by not overeating. I learned I did not have to be obese if I did not want to be. I learned that exercise leads to strength and energy.

I completed three half-marathons. Mind you, I did not win any races, but I completed them.

I learned that women of a certain age have more power and determination than they think they do, and that age and heredity and genes may contribute to healthiness, but they are not the only determinants.

I learned that just because I can carry something well, doesn't mean I should be toting it. Nope. Not at all. I re-learned the truth that no matter how sincerely I believe a lie, it's still a lie.

Living honestly, especially when no one is peering over your shoulder, takes courage. And a good friend or two. I may add my lost forty pounds back over time, but I know I can send them packing again, if I really want to.

"To thine own self be true," is only part of the quote. Shakespeare added, "And it must follow, as the night the day, thou canst not then be false to any man." Not even to yourself.

What lies are you telling yourself?

What one thing can you do to cultivate better health?

Do dragonflies lie?

The Power of the Tease

I believe in the power of the tease. I grew up being teased, and, therefore, I tease a lot. I mean *A Lot,* capital A, capital L, etc. Joking is a time-honored, family tradition passed down from generation to generation in my family.

It is also known to us as *"pickin'."* As in "she's just pickin' on you." We're of the distinct prankster lineage. It's in our DNA, and we are proud of it.

Our pranks and teasings and witty comebacks, puns and plays on words have gotten many of us in trouble in a myriad of ways. In various grades, in sundry schools, teachers thought we talked too much and accused us of attempting to be class clowns. At work, some of our jokes fell short of their goals. In church? Well, for each of the teasings that missed its mark, we've had to ask forgiveness.

Not everyone is used to playfulness with words. Not everyone gets our sense of humor.

I've learned over the years that picking and teasing have their limits and there is a fine line between being mean and taking a tease too far. It isn't that we intend to be mean, it's that the teasing and witty word play and pokin' fun get us carried away and then, in a nano second, what we say is not funny. Over the fine line we go and we tumble into mean town.

A good tease lightens the mood and breaks the ice.

The wrong tease, or one tease too many, runs the risk of harming relationships and causing pain.

I am learning not everyone thinks I'm as funny as I think I am.

When he was four years old, my first-born grandson told me, "Nana, if I'm not laughing, it's not funny." *Ouch.* I remember that. God knows we need our more sensitive kin folk, because those of us who are more calloused don't have a right to just keep on with the picking.

My grandkids tell me I tease too much. I play too much. Poke them in their sides too much. These days I need a backspace key for my mouth, a rewind button for my ears, and a big ole' bottle of *"Wite Out"* ® to erase the misplaced barbs. God forbid I should lose my control key.

Anna Quindlen, in *"A Short Guide to a Happy Life,"* said, "Realize life is glorious, and that you have no business taking it for granted. Care so deeply about goodness that you want to spread it around. Take the money you would have spent on beers in a bar and give it to charity... All of us want to do well. But if we do not do good, too, then doing well will never be enough."

I understand the need for dress rehearsals, but we rarely get to try out our stand-up routines before they just come up and out. We learn to understand the power of the tease, and we must use it wisely.

How playful are you?

When was the last time you were hurt by a joke?

It always helps to reflect
Lake City, South Carolina Lake Park

Keeping My Mind on My Mat

I've been practicing a little yoga. I find it a smooth way to increase flexibility, strengthen, de-stress, and tone. If you're a runner, a walker, or are avoiding the scooter, stretches such as those practiced in yoga are helpful. Useful. Maybe even necessary.

I find there are things learned in the yoga room that I have begun to carry into my life outside the yoga room, which may be part of the plan in practicing yoga.

For me, yoga is a series of poses or postures. That makes me think of "posers," people who are not what they seem or who cannot do what they think.

I believe authenticity is paramount. Living authentically, honestly, true to one's self, with trustworthiness, that is living. So, while I "pose" in a particular "posture" in yoga, I remind myself not to "pose" outside of class. Be who I am, wherever I am.

Yoga is movements of the body, stretches of the limbs. By making the prescribed movements and stretches, bodies de-stress. Re-align. My stretched body becomes a more relaxed one. Stretching is good for my soul. I lean into the stretch. The stretch supports me.

While practicing yoga, we are told not to judge others' movements. Do not criticize yourself, either, for not seeming to be able to do what someone else can do. We are to listen to our bodies and keep our minds on our mats. I am only responsible for me.

Sounds a lot like "Judge not, so that you are not judged," and "Mind your own business," life lessons already employed outside the class. Staying focused on my mat makes me responsible for my poses, for my movements, for me bettering me.

There is talk in yoga of being grounded before one "strikes a pose." Being grounded enables a body to better do whatever is being asked of it. Proper grounding is essential for living life well.

There is talk in the yoga classroom about returning to the "heart center." I believe the heart is the center for what my mind, and body, does. My heart leads me into stretching, urging me to become more flexible. My heart sends oxygen and blood on its way to lead me into being stronger. I breathe slowly, with and through my movements.

I stay in the present moment. I work on becoming more balanced. Grounded. And I stay on my mat.

There is planking for improved muscle tone, and sun salutations for strength and endurance. Downward dogs, upward dogs, and three-legged dogs that help build upper-body strength. There is crocodile, cobra, the chair pose, and more to discover.

I'm working on maintaining an authentic posture, the one that can only come out of my centered being.

What makes you stronger?

Where do you gain your grounding?

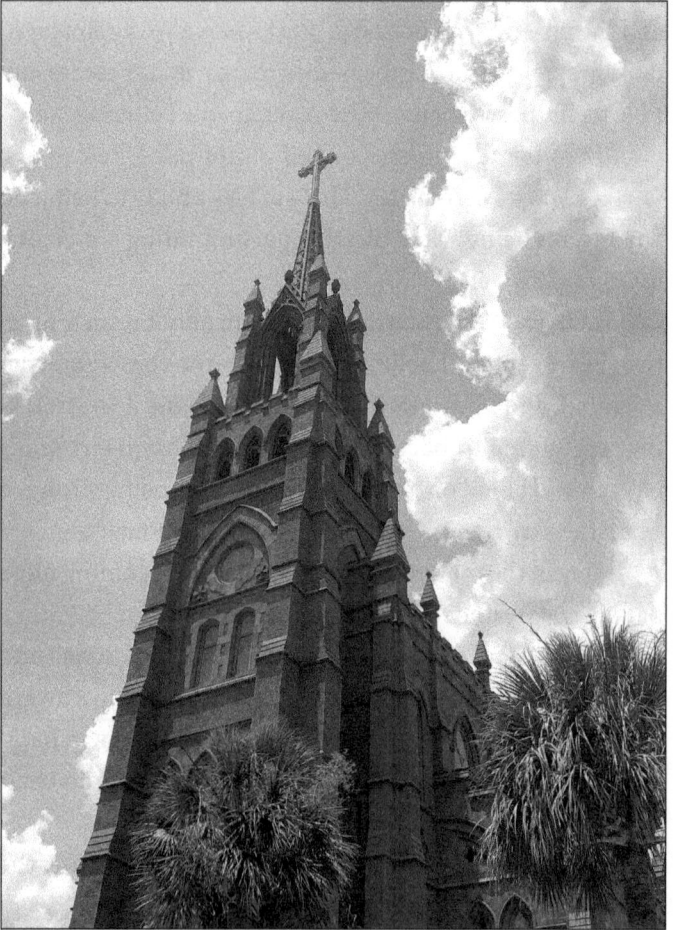

Make a stand

Standing Room Only

For a couple of years now I've taken to standing when I work at my computer and sitting when I am reading or researching. It breaks up the workday and causes me to rise and sit. I read an article in an issue of Runner's World magazine, written by Selene Yeager, that started with "There's no running away from it: the more you sit, the poorer your health and the earlier you may die, no matter how fit you are."

What choice did I really have? I had to take a stand.

The article was entitled *"Is Sitting the New Smoking?"* What a bad endorsement.

Coming from a long line of tobacco farmers, I know what tar and nicotine look like on your hands. I knew I didn't want that black, gummy stuff, coupled with some other things thrown in for good measure during the manufacturing of cigarettes, to pass over my lips and into my lungs. I've seen folks suffer from lung cancer. I have no use for any of the "C" words—not cigarettes or cigars, not catastrophe or calamity, and certainly not cancer.

I simply have little use for something that is as damaging to my health as a tobacco product, but I live by the other "C" word: my computer and what it, and I with it, can do. If you work on a computer, surf the web, play a game, do research or type on a keyboard, or use your cell phone for much of the same, most likely you are sitting. If you watch television, most likely you are sitting. If you're answering telephones and pushing paperwork around on your desk, you're likely sitting. If you're writing, whether on a keyboard or a notepad, you are most likely sitting.

Bottom line, I felt convicted about sitting so much. After reading the article, I decided I needed to put more moving into my days. Of my twenty-four hour day, I figured I sleep about eight of it. That leaves me with about sixteen hours. Between

I watch the news on TV for about an hour when I get up each morning, but I'm usually walking around and listening to it rather than sitting and watching it. And now, I stand or walk or pace or move about for the next four or so hours.

Then I sit for lunch and take a break for an hour or so. Then I'm back at it. On my feet, until by the time five or six o'clock come around again, I'm ready to sit for two or three hours.

Rather than moving being an exception, which it had become, I've built it into my day. I think that's the way it's supposed to be. While I have no empirical data to say I may not be better for standing, I'm sure I'm not any worse for it either.

I do feel I have more energy and I do believe that now when I sit, I'm actually at rest, instead of antsy and fidgeting.

If my days are numbered no matter what I do, then this may just be a futile attempt on my part to entice my

Maker to be more pleased with me. "Look, over here. I'm trying. See me standing? I'm the one waving my arms and not resting on my laurels. Pick me last!"

I believe we are created to walk, run, lift, tote, fetch, push, pull and move, and I also believe that we don't. Life is easier for us than it needs to be. I have chosen to pick up the pace a little. I may not be able to do anything to offset the timing of my death, but I'll stand up while trying.

What makes you feel more energetic?

What do you stand for?

Windows in South Carolina's Charleston

Luck and the Prepared

What do you learn while making preparations for a coming emergency? Do you live in tornado alley? On a storm-ridden coast? Felt a tremor? Lived through a fire, landslide, earthquake, or hurricane? We should all be prepared for our next disaster.

If you have your umbrella, it is less likely to rain than if you don't. I believe that. My husband laughs at me because there are four umbrellas of various sizes and styles in my car. One for each potential passenger.

I believe luck favors the prepared. I also believe luck can run out but am trusting in God that it will not.

"Did you ever observe to whom accidents happen?" chemist Dr. Louis Pasteur is reported to have asked in 1854. He added, "In the fields of observation, fortune (chance in the vernacular of today) favors the prepared mind." So there it is, scientifically supported. Staying prepared will, in all likelihood, give you better luck. Trusting in God, the great equalizer, will get you to the other side of any disaster.

Pasteur's *"prepared mind"* quote has always inspired me. His contributions to science, technology, and medicine are astounding. He developed the method of pasteurization of wine and milk and the rabies vaccination. We'd be sicker without him.

He worked to make the world a safer, more prepared and therefore luckier place. He led the movement in the medical community to acknowledge and accept that germs exist.

Here, after the one attributed to Pasteur, are the other six of my top seven preparedness quotes.

6. *"Depend on the rabbit's foot if you will, but remember it didn't work for the rabbit."* R.E. Shay

5. *"Diligence is the mother of good luck."* Benjamin Franklin

4. *"The only sure thing about luck is that it will change."* Wilson Mizner (Though others may be credited in today's world, I credit him.)

3. *"Fortune brings in some boats that are not steered."* William Shakespeare

2. *"Good luck is another name for tenacity of purpose."* Ralph Waldo Emerson

1. *"Ability is of little account without opportunity."* Lucille Ball

How's your luck?

Where's your umbrella?

Perpetual praying is preparation

Grieving

This grief is hanging out after closing time. This grief keeps stealing away my breath.

I was resigned when Granddaddy George died. Cancer. Death was his only way to get better.

I was transported to some new place beyond anger when Granddaddy Jim died. Where was the miracle he was due?

Grandma Lee was less difficult to let go of. She always said this world was not her home. She slipped away into life everlasting.

Grandmamma Addie's big ole' heart gave out. She passed from here to there with her sister near her. She moved beyond us.

I have marked time by these four deaths. "That was just after he died." "She was born three months after she died."

Until now.

Some say the loss of a mother is the heaviest grief to carry. Some things I just do not want to know.

Death of a spouse? Just take me first. Death of a child? I do not dare imagine.

Once upon a time God brought my dad back from a trip to the edge. He was near dead after his head-on collision with the trees on a foggy fall morning.

Bliss. He was back.

One October, though, The Creator whisked Daddy away in the early afternoon, stole him from his recliner, took him before help could arrive. We had no time to pray. No time to bargain.

They said he'd had a heart attack. I say we are having heart attacks.

To get through the visitation of family and friends, I settled on a formal portrait of him and my mom on the table across the room from me. He smiles at me all evening, through the sea of people and plants. This is no good goodbye.

We celebrated his birthday on Friday and mourned him on Tuesday. There is solace in the remembrances of him.

At his house, home, I pretend he is taking a long trip. At my house, I place the portrait of him on the bookshelf. It lands beside *Jumping Hurdles, Hitting Glitches and Overcoming Setbacks.* I see the message. He reads, make that past tense, read, westerns.

I am empty. I am see-through.

What got me through once doesn't help me today. I cannot, do not look at your smile. I don't want you to smile at me. Everything is not okay.

Water drips off my chin. Death is the most real part of life.

I know better than to be surprised when people die. Death doesn't care how old, ready, or willing we are, to go or let go. Death doesn't care how many unfinished projects there are. Death is and was and will be.

You can't avoid people when you're grieving. Not all of them say the right thing. I forgive them.

I have more questions to ask. Tell me the story of the rolling store, the man and his wagon and the home goods, again. You stole the man's chickens? And sold them back to him? Where'd he come from? Georgetown?

Family was number one for him. His vice—cigarettes. His passion—hound dogs, the finest fox-hunting hound dogs.

This grief is hanging out long, long after closing time.

Have you practiced writing your obituary?

Is there something beyond this world?

Alone With Memories
Alex Palkovich, Sculptor
Florence Veterans Park, South Carolina

The Possible

I have endured and come out on the other side of what I thought at the time was impossible. I was naïve and said, "I can't possibly do this." And I did.

I was immature and thought, "I will not go through this again." But I have.

I was ignorant and screamed, "I do not have the ability, strength, or desire to continue." Yet I will.

I did. I have. I will. Experience tells me I can.

I will. I do, even if begrudgingly. Because I must. That which does not kill me makes me stronger, right? Nietzsche, the German philosopher, wrote that before losing all his mental capacities. There is that in us that has the will to power, he said.

I motor on, doing the possible.

What are you motoring through that you thought you could not?

Where has your motoring on taken you?

For as long as I can, I will

Slow Thaw

Cold breaks
young twigs
bold branches
and old limbs.
There is music in the cracking.
Cold breaks us all.
Await the slow thaw.

The Fowler Dining Room
The International Culinary Institute of Myrtle Beach
Restaurant Capstone Class

Split Pea Soup in Winter

A Good Ride

Somewhere between there, where I was, say, on King Avenue because that's where my recollections begin (though I've seen photographs of what came before), and here, in my home in Hannah, I have learned a thing or two about that and this.

Living is a journey. Life is a gift. I didn't ask for it. It happened to me. I happened to my parents. I became an individual and was plopped onto the moving sidewalk of life, all totally unbeknownst to me. One day I wasn't. A few moments later, I was.

My ride home from the clinic where I was born in the afternoon was in a hearse. In small towns and in former times, such as it was, vehicles pulled double duty. It was also the ambulance. My mom held me. My dad followed behind in the family car. We went to my great uncle's house where my grandmother was living. We stayed so we could be looked after until it was time for Mamma to resume her duties in her home, in another house on this same farm.

Do you know your birth story?

Once my legs were strong enough to support my head and arms and such, and the second my feet were willing, I was propelled to smell, go, do, see, taste, touch and hear, and all that smelling, going, doing, seeing, tasting, touching, and hearing led me to cultivating and accumulating. Over time, I refined my cultivating and accumulating, and some of my discoveries were discarded and abandoned. I fled. I hid. Really, I hid.

I loved hiding in closets, under beds, and once my head got stuck between the wall and the washing machine. I always pushed the limits on tight spaces, wondering "Will I fit?"

What funny story can you tell about yourself?

I trusted and doubted. I learned to say "please" and "thank you" and I've learned that I'm not very fond of it when others don't.

We grow, mature, change, and if we are among the fortunate, we learn, adapt, and flourish. We adopt. We cherish pets, people, places, and particles. We cultivate. We are who we are, going where we're going, doing what we do.

Each hour of life is filled with sitting and staying, watching and being. I am often filled with twitching and twittering, hiding and finding.

I have as my computer's desktop background a screenshot of a photograph of a meme. The meme is a cartoon of two goofy-looking characters. One stands with his arms folded tightly across his stomach while asking the second one a question.

"Why so optimistic about 2019? What do you think it will bring? Everything seems so messed up." (In this case the year is 2019, but you can fill it in with the year of your choice.)

Goofy-looking character Two replies, "I think it will bring flowers."

"Yes? How come?" One asks, to which Two says, "Because I'm planting flowers."

Indeed, that is what goofy character Two is drawn doing. He has a hand trowel, seeds, and is digging in the dirt with the water can close at hand.

Goofy character Two could leave the flowers to chance. A few might bloom. But by purposefully cultivating, and planting, he hedges his bets that there will be flowers. I want flowers. I plant them. I want others to have flowers, so I share them.

The questions are *Where are you going?* and *What are you cultivating?*

My last ride in life, most likely, will be just like my first. I will be taken away in a hearse. I will go out as I came in.

I know I will have had a good ride. You can bet on it.

How did you spend your day yesterday?

How will you spend your time tomorrow, if given the chance?

It's time to learn to make a basket.
Do this in the company of friends.

Illumination

I've only talked to Antwan once. He was telling his story to a group of men and women, just a few years younger than he, offering to give them hope if they would listen. And try. Things take effort. And hard work. Persistence.

Some tuned in to hear him. Others stared at their telephones and twiddled their thumbs.

In the beginning, Antwan didn't think he was anything special. He thought when he graduated high school that maybe he could work in the local grocery store. He saw enough in the world, though, to think that maybe, just maybe, he could be more.

In fact, there were those around him in that grocery store who thought he could likely one day even manage a grocery store. Oh, he managed all right. He became something despite those who thought he was already what he could be.

Today, Antwan is a political pundit, a sought-after commentator with his finger on the pulse of national elections. He and his thoughts are invited to dinner, asked out after events. His insights are requested. He is a helper, seer, and doer.

Sam Nunn. Maybe you've heard of him, maybe you haven't. A politician from Georgia. I was covering one of his reelection campaigns in the 1980s for a small newspaper. There was something about Nunn—his choice of words, his character, the way he reasoned things out, the way he listened—that made those in his presence smarter.

Politicians and their makers come and go. Some stay far longer than they are useful. They have their seat at the table set for two: us, and them. There is always room for more seats at the table.

Standing next to Antwan, listening, I saw the soul behind those eyes. It was keen, quick-witted and seeking, always taking in, learning and synthesizing. He put together the at-odds pieces in the world and created plausible outcomes in the swirl of the meeting of opposing thoughts and words.

Antwan told the story of a woman who'd lived to be at least one hundred and eight-years-old, who had taught herself to read by using the Sears and Roebuck catalog. He explained how reading opens the doors to life.

"It's not where you start, but where you end," he said. "Use your time wisely," he said. "Take advantage of every resource that comes your way." Antwan said he'd had more bills than money when he graduated college and he couldn't get toilet tissue with his credit score, but he persevered.

"Not only do we work for a seat at the table," Antwan said. "But work to build a bigger table. Bring more folks with us." Open seating, everyone is invited.

"And whatever you do, don't pass the torch," Antwan said. "Let the next person get their light from your torch, and you keep running."

Cultivating

Pass the light, not the torch. Carry the torch so the light is passed to others who carry new torches and lights.

Imagine the illumination.

Did someone pass you a torch or the light?

What are you passing on to those who come behind you?

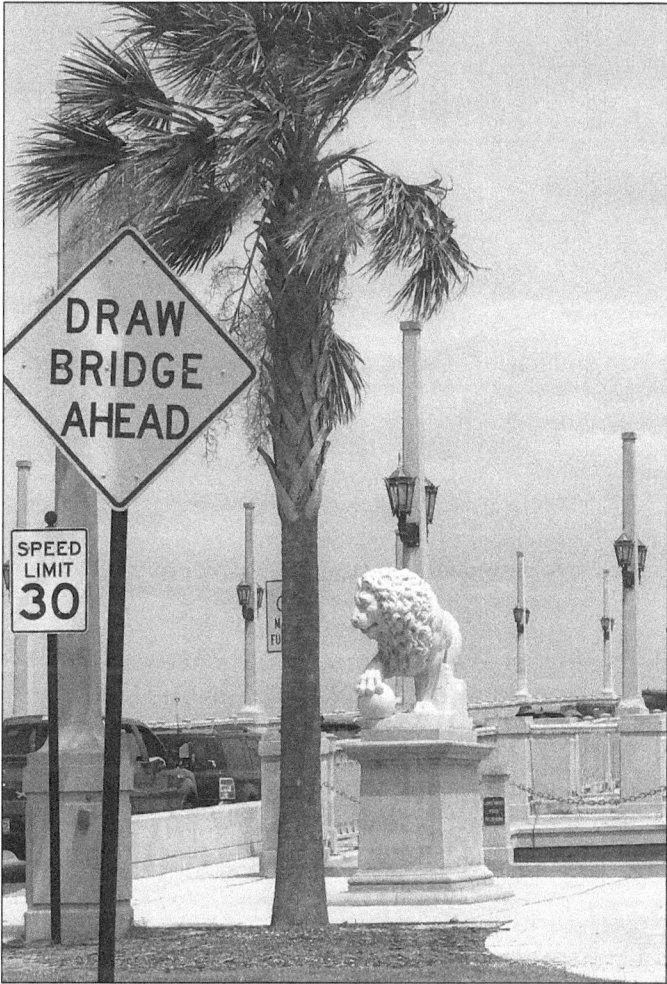

There will be obstacles. There will be traffic.
But go forward anyway.

Dream Weaver

Wonky, wonky Dream Weaver.
You gave me another's dream.

Mismatched. Misaligned. Wrong way on a one way.

I know no one in this dream;
Foreigners each.

Someone must have my images.
The one that revisits, about the big house.

Or the running through the field looking for my hat.
That one was mine for sure.

Bring them back to me,
Wonky, wonky Dream Weaver.

Set a trap. Weave away.

Way-Staying

Way-staying is not yet a word, that I know of, although, maybe in some places, by some people in some countries and cultures, it is a real thing. Maybe in some languages there is one word that means "staying along the way." But it should be a word. Here's why.

In the years following 2008, after the economic crumbling of the world's economies, many were forced out of their homes. Foreclosures, we call them. Some became street people, adding to the numbers of those already enduring the harsh life of making a home in a car or a box, in worst case scenarios, or in a shelter run by do-gooders in best-case scenarios. Or maybe those shelters are not best cases and the box is preferable. I'd want a tent. I'd also want it to be waterproof, but as the great recession showed us, we don't always get what we want.

Families were given the boot because they fell behind in their mortgage payments and were falling behind in keeping up with the Joneses, whoever they are. The displaced became way-stayers, temporarily living wherever they could, most likely in a series of other people's homes, typically making use of improvised sleeping arrangements. The sun porch, the bonus room above the garage, the guest room, formal dining room, each converted to allow the others a place to rest, where they could catch their breath.

Far too many people were left homeless and have been couch surfing ever since with parents or friends. Sometime before 2010, I heard a radio show announcer discussing this trend. I know the trend has not yet ended. It occurs to me that couch-surfing, road-tripping, wayfaring, and way-staying are real, tangible things. Those who could, cashed out, bought some type of camper, and took to the campgrounds and roads. The others sought refuge where they could find it.

John Lawson was an English explorer, naturalist, and writer. He was instrumental in the mapping of the interior of colonial North Carolina, South Carolina, and Georgia. The announcer was discussing the publishing of his expeditions in a book. He founded two settlements in North Carolina; one is Bath, the other New Bern, both located on rivers in the coastal plain of North Carolina. This is the person the radio announcer was discussing. These are my places, my people, and my interest was piqued.

In the history books, Lawson is remembered as an explorer, naturalist, and writer. He was also an opportunist, adventurer, traveler, pioneer, wayfarer, and way-stayer. Wayfaring is traveling by foot. Way-staying was the art of getting strangers to let you stay with them along your way.

Perhaps there was an introduction letter he carried in his left breast pocket. "This man is worthy of your food and home," it might have read. Perhaps he was enigmatic and charismatic. Perhaps he brought gifts from one place to another, a sort of bribe for a night's stay. Perhaps people were attuned to those traveling and needing accommodations. So, staying from home to home he did, telling stories of what he'd seen and inquiring where to go next.

The next time a friend asks to crash on your couch for "just a day or two, until I can make arrangements/get back on my feet," think of yourself as entertaining a wayfarer. By the 1850s the term "way station" was used in America to refer to stops along the way (think of along the stage coach route), often offering supplies as well as a place to crash for the night.

We are born of travelers. We think we invent things, such as couch surfing in the twenty-first century. Really, though, we just reinvent what is needed in the here and now. And relive the past without knowing it.

What are you busy reinventing?

What would you like to invent?

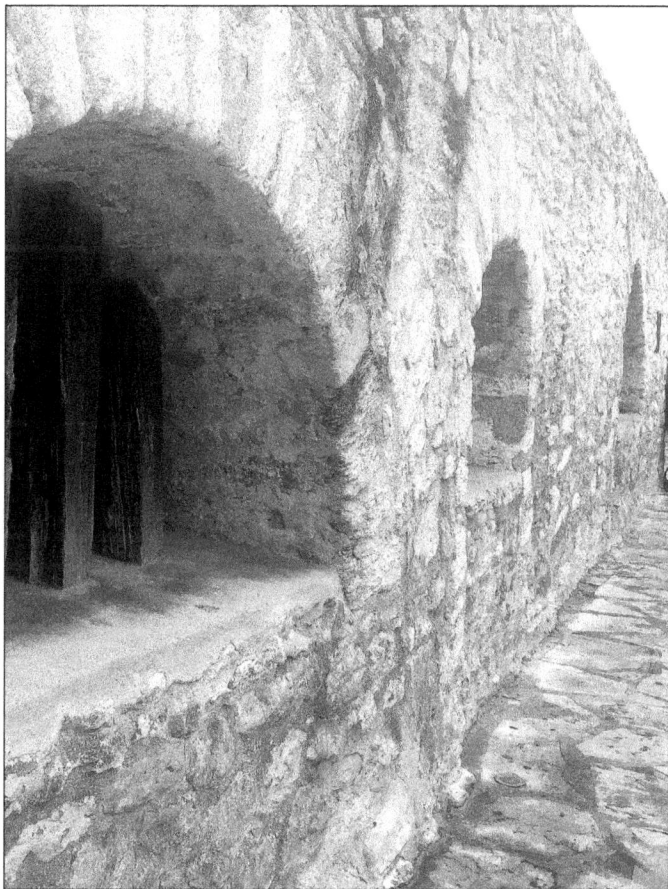

Wall of the Convento of the Alamo, San Antonio, Texas
Where once some people stayed.

All in the Timing

Doors open in. Doors swing out.
Time whistles through.
Insane, profane, inane, seeking to sustain ...
Guzzling, never quenching the thirst for more.
What goes in must come out.
Conjuring a feud, backward, forward,
the passing mood, a song hummed just off key.
Listen.
Hinges ask the question, reply.
Ask the question, reply.
The song slips through. Vines grown
by time wrap the song.
This too shall pass.

From living trees, to logs, to planks.

Getting a New View

This scene has been captured in photographs and in the minds of those who looked out this doorway and onto this dirt lane since the late 1800s. The lane served as the way to the fields and homes dotting the woods to the swamp where fishing and trapping for food was the norm.

Those houses are gone, except the one left dying. New homes have sprouted.

Instead of a livelihood from crops of cotton, corn and tobacco, the fields produce fodder for deer, rabbit, and turkey. The diminished swamp and the river beyond are lessened by drought, dams, and diversions. Though changed, they are, for now, still present.

The fish and ducks that frequented the Lynches River have been relocated by time and necessity. Change, though she comes in many forms, is always with us. She holds our hands as we try to out-run her, and sometimes drags us along in her footsteps. The hard-top road, the one that did not exist for hundreds of years and then magically was, is being reborn.

Progress is moving this old tobacco-packing house to another site, and this view will be lost forever. That is what I'm thinking as I dangle my feet over the edge of the top doorway of the two-story barn. This view, out this doorway from this perch, no longer exists. Nonexistent.

But all is not lost. The elderly packing house has found a new home, with new views awaiting the brave who climb the rickety stairs. Salute! I will not grieve for views lost, but eagerly await views not yet seen and scenes yet to be written.

What do you see out of your favorite window?

How would you feel if the view changed?

1862 West Highway 378-Hannah, January 1, 2014

My Mamma Said

When they were younger, I told my girls if they didn't want to go somewhere or be with someone and they couldn't just say "no" or "no, thank you," to use me as their excuse.

"My mamma said I have to be home at midnight."

"My mamma said I can't go this weekend."

"My mamma said you're not a good influence on me."
Okay, that one probably never actually was said, but it was the whole intent of the blaming things on Mamma. I had their backs and I was their excuse. Still am.

I'm not sure I want to know what all I got blamed for. But I know I am glad my girls could blame me for caring enough to want the best for them. I feared they would give in and go along with the crowds, not that the crowds were bad. Crowd-think can make a person lose valuable time, time wasted on chasing others' dreams and desires.

I wanted/want them to drag other people along with them, not to be dragged along. They are the leaders.

I know I still have my mamma's words all too often in my head. And, if not in my head, in my emails, such as this one from more than ten years ago.

From: rdsha@xyz.net
Sent: Tuesday, July 21, 2009 3:10 PM
To: Owens, Dianne P.
Subject:

> Read your blog and as usual was well worded and written with the style, finesse and professionalism of a true journalist. One who is talented and I feel will have a lot of success in the future. In replying to the last section of your quoting Emerson, my life has been better and happier because of you. you are a wonderful and special Daughter, and I am very proud of you and your gift of writing. never doubt your ability to make the written word come alive and it to be an inspiration to someone.. My prayers are with as you enter this new phase (or chapter) of your life.

> Love…Mama

Thank you. I haven't forgotten your words. Did I tell you about the time my mamma stopped what she was doing and put me first? When we disagree, as we sometimes do, being the headstrong, independent women we have been raised to be, I conjure up these memories.

You can't argue with someone when you picture them playing yard games with you. She played hopscotch with me just a time or two, but that was enough. She taught me how to jump a rope, a game meant for at least three people, when you only have two.

It was just a few months after we had moved into our new neighborhood. I was eight and had not yet made friends. It was a warm summer night. She was cooking dinner and the window over the kitchen sink was open.

Occasionally she'd talk to me through the screen. I was bored. I drew a hopscotch game in our grassless yard and asked her to play with me. Hopscotch is better when played with others. And she did. Another time, when I complained that it was tough being the only girl among brothers who didn't care about jumping rope, she came outside, tied one end of the rope to the doorknob of an outside door, and taught me hold the rope. And to jump. She also took time to turn the rope so I could jump.

She stopped doing what she needed to do to help me do what I wanted to do. When I had no one to spend time with, she was there. My mamma said I was important, and that's all that matters.

How often do you show encouragement to others?

Whose back do you have?

Giraffe in Riverbanks Zoo
Columbia, South Carolina

Forgiveness

Once upon a time our dog Rascal was barking out back. My husband went to investigate and found a raccoon. Raccoons can carry rabies, so he went to get the rifle to shoot it and take the corpse to Environmental Services so they could test it for rabies.

At the shot, Rascal bolted. He didn't come for quite a time. In fact, it was the end of the day by the time he slowly came up out of the woods along the swamp, as if to say, "You all right, man?"

He judged my husband harshly. From Rascal's perspective, I suppose, his best friend in the whole wide world was behaving irrationally. His best response to the situation was to get out of Dodge while the gettin' was good.

To his credit, Rascal returned home, even if a little shell-shocked. He had no way of knowing the shooting had nothing to do with him.

Thankfully, at least with pets, forgiveness is always possible.

What is your favorite pet story?

To whom do you owe forgiveness?

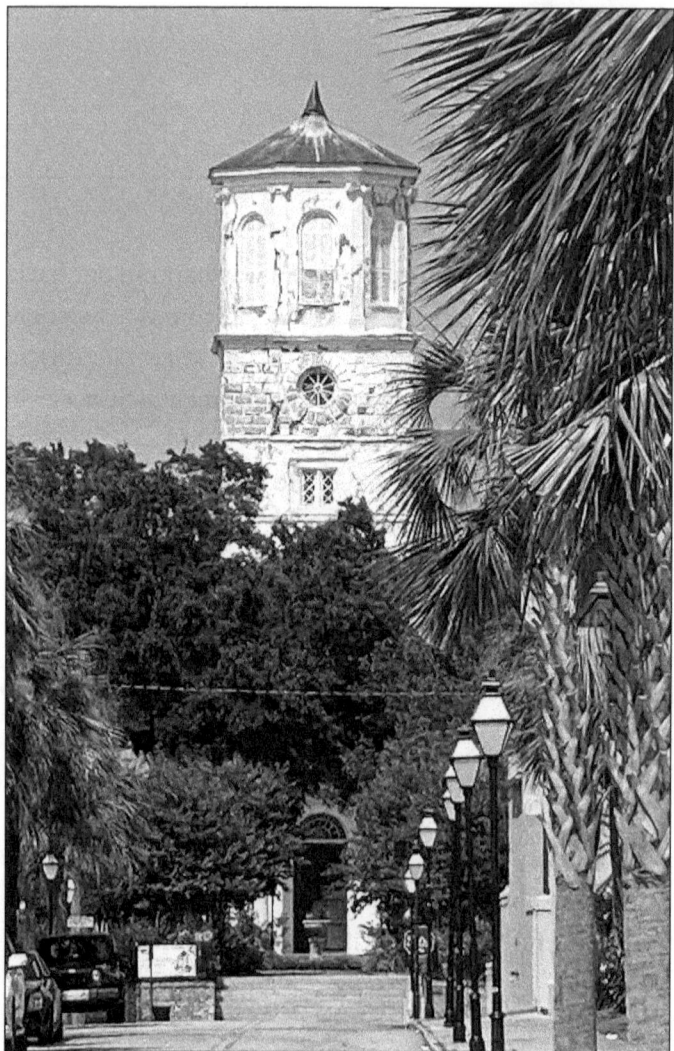

A place of forgiveness
Charleston, South Carolina

The Beauty of a Cup of Tea

It may be tea time any time for many, but for me, a cup of tea is the only answer to a dreary, rainy day.

Ruled by my taste buds, I'm a coffee drinker—morning, noon, afternoon, night. Mostly black and warm, the coffee in my cup has been known to be hot, cold, sweet, and milky. It's an automatic thing for me to walk into the kitchen of a home and assess what kind of people live there.

Coffee pot? No coffee pot? Small, four-cup coffee maker? Twelve-cup coffee maker? When I find a coffee maker mounted under a kitchen cabinet, I know I've found a kindred spirit of the coffee kind.

Sometimes, though, when it's rainy and dreary or foggy and chilly, I want a cup of hot tea. I steep my leaves in a teapot and pour up a cup or two. There are times coffee will not suffice. Coffee doesn't help you shake such a chill in the air. That's the beauty of a cup of tea.

Many folks living in my part of the world drink their tea poured over ice and sweetened so their teeth slowly rot after each glass. I'm not sure when I last enjoyed tea made that way. I do know that I lost the taste, and desire, for cold, sweet tea.

We recently had a week or two of sunless, dreary, Seattle-like days. It would have been easy to forget which coast my state clings to had my GPS not constantly reminded me when traveling that I am next to the Atlantic. Warm tea became a necessity for surviving those grey days.

Along with the steeping, pouring and teacup or mug selecting, I allowed myself to remember hundreds of tea parties I've enjoyed over the years, the fancy and planned, the simple and impromptu.

I can drink from the brown cup that was Aunt Mable's or the shorter, rounder one with roses, a cup from Grandmamma Addie's china. There's a fancy teacup, a gift from Jackie; a slender mug from Mary, complete with a steeping lid.

Whether it was the tea or the weather that made me reminiscent I cannot be sure. But there he was, my step-grandfather from England. I saw his smile, heard him joking with me and wanted to touch the wave in his black hair.

He once gave me a lesson in self-defense in his tiny living room. I was going away to college. He knew fighting moves. Each summer he worked shirtless and tanned until his skin was the color of a Greek tycoon who spent the days on his yacht. His sister Gladys enjoyed afternoon teas and taught me much about the taking of the tea tradition, how to keep the pot, and thus the tea, warm and the proper "biscuit" to serve.

Warmed by memories, I could feel the sun shining— somewhere. That's the beauty of a cup of tea. It takes you to wherever you need to be.

How do you face gray, otherwise yucky days?

What do you do that conjures good memories?

Tea time tends the soul

Pancakes and Butterflies

Daughter number one picks up her oldest child in his second week of kindergarten to discover he has his first loose tooth. She seeks to console him and tells him this is a good thing.

She explains that when the tooth comes out, they will wrap it in tissue, place it under the pillow in his bed and the Tooth Fairy will replace it with money during the night.

There is silence in back seat of the car as the five-year-old begins processing this information. He asks, "Can the Tooth Fairy leave money and my tooth?"

"No, honey, the tooth fairy wants your tooth, she pays for it."

"Mommy," he replies, "That's gross!"

More silence, and then: "Will this be Tooth Fairy money or human money?"

Laughing, my daughter replies from the front seat, "Honey, it will be human money you can use to buy something at the store."

More silence, then as the car turns into the driveway at home comes "I need to talk about this with my Daddy!"

Now, whether the child didn't believe or trust his mom, I can't say. Whether he preferred fairy money to human, I can only surmise. Truth is, though, neither he nor his sister have enjoyed the idea of a tooth-buying fairy coming into their rooms at night while they sleep.   His sister makes her parents sleep with the tooth under one of their pillows. Even if it's a well-meaning tooth-buying fairy, it is leaving money under someone else's pillow, not hers.

Daughter number two and her son are visiting a new church. In the lobby is a small table with handouts that advertise the church-sponsored Cub Scout troop. The daughter is very excited and begins to explain to her six-year-old that she wants him to get involved in scouting, as she has fond memories of camping, canoeing, and hiking with her father as a child.

"Your grandfather was an Eagle Scout," she proudly announced.

Wide-eyed, her son asked, "Does Papa still hunt birds?"

Not everyone is excited about a fairy coming into their room at night. Not everyone knows what an Eagle Scout is. The job each day is to seek to understand and be understood.

A butterfly is not a fly made of butter, and a dragon fly is not a dragon at all, but, thankfully, a pancake is indeed a thin, flat cake of batter turned and fried on each side in a pan.

What have you heard a child say that made you think twice?

When did you last believe in something outside of what you can see?

A butterfly is anything but butter

Car Therapy

Sometimes you need a little a car therapy.

If you grew up learning to drive as soon as your feet could hit the brake, which is way more important than pushing the gas pedal, then sometimes you need to take a drive. Learning to make appropriate stops helps avoid a myriad of problems later, I assure you. But back to car therapy.

If you don't drive, but walk wherever you need to go, then these thoughts may be a stretch for you. Perhaps, though, they will help you to get up and just go, get out and just be. That's the gist of things.

Driving is soul cleansing. You recognize the need to just get away. Go. Windows down, hair blown, music loud. Sometimes, it's just round and round the roundabout. Sometimes it's to the top of the parking garage and back down again. Doesn't have to take long. Don't have to go far.

This drive does not *always* require speed. Sometimes, forty-five miles per hour is fast enough. It all depends on what we are running from or to. The need for speed wrestles with the need for safety.

Let's say the boss yelled at you. The kids think you're mean. Or you're tired of the same four walls. Take the drive.

Let the pain wash over you. Let the anger free to the wind. Scream. Yell. This vehicle is safe space.

Give voice to the fears and the what-ifs. Talk it out. Shout them down.

Car therapy is best accompanied by a soundtrack. Prince's "Little Red Corvette," Bob's "Against the Wind," Bruce's "Born to Run," or Elton and B-B-B-Bennie and the Jets.

And then there are the times when only Pink, Reba, Aretha, Whitney, or Barbra will do.

In the car I do battle with real and imaginary enemies and have conversations with living and dead friends. I pray for the Almighty to intervene and for myself to relinquish control and we all begin to have realistic expectations.

I let the road lead. It always takes me home again.

Where do you go when you need to ride?

When was the last time you went somewhere new?

Highway 378, looking west

Yesterday's Cup

Hello yesterday's cup of coffee! So, this is where you hid from me for the past twenty-four hours? Did you not hear me yesterday call to you? Oh, wait, you're the cup that hid from me two days ago. I remember now. I set this cup down to make a telephone call and then left the room to wander around the house as I talked. Thanks for waiting on me to come back. But let's find yesterday's coffee and toss the both of you.

That's a good synopsis of many of my days. I pour the cup of steaming coffee, take a sip or two, place the cup on a bookcase, window ledge, coffee table, or in an open cabinet while I reach for something on the shelf and, well, eventually, after searching a while, I pour myself a fresh cup.

It is a good day when I rediscover my lost cup before the coffee is tepid. No matter, even if tepid, I will drink it.

And so it goes. My coffee cups. They don't wander, as I once supposed, from place to place trying to play a game of hide-and-seek with me. There is no coffee fairy to take the cup and place it elsewhere. Nor do the cups of coffee chase me from place to place trying to keep up with me when it's clear I've left them behind in my daily doings.

They clearly stay put, lazy little things, wherever I place them. I suppose after a few minutes they stop wondering about me and begin feeling a little neglected, left behind as they are, supplanted by some other thought, idea, need or want. In the end, I fear they fear they are forgotten.

It's that way with misplaced things. They stay put. We move on. The great thing about yesterday's cup is that eventually we meet up again. Nothing is ever truly lost. It is just where it is, waiting on the finding.

What do you have trouble keeping up with?

How do you like your coffee?

Beans of life

First, Walk with Me

One tall, one shorter, one dark, the other lighter. One, long-legged in blue jeans and sneakers, keeping time with the other, in yoga pants, tank-topped and wearing ballet-like slippers. Two step. The two were in step. Walking, together.

Matching steps, each laughed, as they shared a sidewalk. The walk is important. If you want to know me, first walk with me. They shared air, space, time, the time it takes to get there. This will be a memory.

Walk with me, let's see where they go. You dance, I'll run; you walk, I'll skip. Together. Different and the same. They, and then we, get to the corner.

Turning right in step, they, and we, soldiers of conversation watch the traffic, careful not to become a casualty. Negotiating curbing, turning here.

Thanks for not letting me walk this path alone, but this is my stop.

You continue ahead; we will meet again. There can be no again, if there is not a first.

First, come, walk with me.

Do you walk alone or together?

What do you see around you when you walk?

Steadfast ant friends
Together, together, always together.

No More Puttin' In

In the late 1800s, growing tobacco became *the* way to make money on my family's farm. Cotton, corn, and beans of several sorts were grown, too, but the cash crop, the money maker, the farm sustainer, was the settin' out and puttin' in of tobacco.

To better sell the ancient crop that grew so well in the soil in the south, tobacco companies earnestly embarked on their overseas marketing plans, increased the types of uses for tobacco, and lobbied, with the farmers, for government support of the crop. It seemed there was nothing that tobacco money couldn't buy. It built churches and schools and homes and houses. It bought clothes and cars and washing machines and paid for college educations.

For me, putting in tobacco referred to the cropping (breaking off of leaves from their stalk), the bringing of those leaves from the field to the barn on a wooden sleigh/wagon pulled behind a tractor, the stringing of those leaves onto an inch-square stick, and the placement of those sticks into the barn, loading the barn poles from the top down. There are older ways and newer ways of bringing the crop to the barn. This is a memory of my youth.

Puttin' in is a second step after settin' out. That's planting. A next step is the drying and curing of the crop by heat.

In the oldest days, this was done by wood-fueled fires, and later by heat generated by burning fuel oil. The heat was forced through flues, metal heat-scattering contraptions. Flue-cured tobacco. Then came the takin' out.

We took the sticks of tobacco out from the barn one by one, loading them back onto the trailer or wagon, and hauling them to a holding or packing house. We unloaded stick after stick of tobacco, the same sticks we had a week or so earlier put into the barn, and transported them to where the tobacco was then taken off the sticks and packed into sheets of coarse burlap for shipping. The hundred-or-so-pound sheets of tobacco were then loaded onto a trailer and taken to market. There, the tobacco was sold by auction to the highest bidder. There is much more to this story. But that's all for now.

Three things: This was hard, repetitive work. It was labor-intensive and needed many people in many places to get the process done properly. If you were surrounded by the right people, it wasn't all bad. There were laughs and jokes and picking and teasing. And a little money at the end of the day.

In 2007 I wrote this **Ode to the Passing of the Tobacco Barn**.

> *The passing of time has made these barns obsolete*
> *The workers who toiled under their shelters forgotten.*
> *The way of life connected to them is just a shadow of a*
> *   memory . . . wrapped in*
> *a sweet tea and hot biscuit at lunch,*

nabs and Red Rocks at break,
and blessed sleep at the end of a very tiring day.

With a dip of his hat the old barn bids adieu to me and you …
Held together by twine, kudzu and wisteria vines,
Logs give way to time tearing them down …
Some just tired of being, some ashamed of what they were.
Log on log, brick on brick, the industry was built
And it went on to build banks and churches and homes and schools.
Only to be forgotten. Hidden. Left to peek out at a new world beyond its reach.
Tobacco barns. Oh the secrets they hide. The laughter, the teasing. Where there was wearisome work in wind and rain.
Sad. Forsaken. Forgotten. Forlorn.
That's the passing of the tobacco barn.

What in your culture has given way to something new?

What do you wish would disappear that hasn't?

My Tobacco Barn

Trusting the Algorithm

Rivers run steady, deep, and wide;
Fresh water springs from the well.
I heard it said there is an arrogance of the algorithm.
We trust that computer more than ourselves.

Computers ought to augment,
that's all,
never supplant human intelligence.

We can figure it out. We have figured it out. We will.
Unless.
AI. Artificial.
Second best. Unreal.

There's always another song to sing, another story to tell.
Unless we trust the algorithm,
more than we trust ourselves.

Turtle in the grass

Profundity

As a reporter, I nearly always got more information than I needed for any given story. It may not have been germane to the story at hand, but information always got filed away in my brain. Being a journalist was/is one of the last great jobs for a generalist. In a world of specialization and smokestacks of information, journalists get to know a lot about a lot of different topics.

One of the hardest stories I ever wrote was the one about SIDS. Before that story, I had no idea that babies died for seemingly no reason. That air passages could so easily give up and that lives could be so quickly changed. I've never forgotten the lost looks in the eyes of the mother and grandmother interviewed. There is no way to properly discuss the death of a child.

No one is equipped for that. No helmet, catcher's mitt, mask, chest protector or leg guards can do the trick of stalling the ache that comes from such a loss. And in the end, always, death is about someone's child.

But there I was, a new mom myself, asking personal questions about a hurt so raw, so recent, though it had been a year or two. The two were starting a support group. They wanted to get the word out. They wanted the opportunity to talk about death. They started by sharing with me what they could. And I shared what was needed to get a story written and for a support group to be born.

To date, for me, there's always been another cup of coffee to drink, another tree to climb, one more piece of pie. But that day I became aware that no matter how much time lapses, and though every day is a new day if you get to have it, some things make coffee taste more bitter, make trees less attractive for an adventure, and make pie lose its flavor.

Profundity.

What do you know that you wish you didn't?

What do you wish you could share that you can't?

Train tracks over the Lynches River
Venter's Landing, Johnsonville, South Carolina

Christmas Parade

Proximity, partnership, personal.
Competent. Practiced.

Make it matter that you came.
Everything changes because you show up.
Contribute. A smile. If not a hand-
shake, a greeting just the same.

In God we live and move and have our being.
Cultivate the collective of learning.

The Drummer
Hemingway High School 2019

The Elephant's Sneeze

I am the girl whom the elephant sneezed on at the zoo. Swung his/her trunk side to side, reared back, and unloaded. It was disgusting. To this day I shudder when I remember it. To be sure, I had my fingers enlaced with the fence surrounding the elephant and my face pressed against it.

Thankfully, I was wearing glasses. It took hot water and soap to remove the sticky goo. It was harder getting that gunk out of my hair. I learned to not stand so close to the elephants.

You may not believe me, but many witnessed it. Some still remind me of it. I've also been pooped on by a bird while sitting in a chair in my backyard.

Consider this your warning: don't stand near me when we're outdoors. These are not my only two run-ins with nature. I was also spit on by a llama. In another encounter, I was stared at by a monkey at the zoo. I turned to look behind me to see what the monkey saw, only to realize I was the species being observed.

I don't let these experiences dissuade me. I still wander in nature. Still visit the zoo, keeping a healthy distance from the elephant and llama. Still go to the beach. Still hike in the mountains.

I've learned to watch for signs. I check the ground for droppings and signs of birds resting in the trees before selecting a spot on the ground for my chair. I tell people there are just some truths you will learn in life. It's best to share the lessons to help others. If they don't heed your lessons, though, let them learn for themselves.

Experience and nature are competent teachers.

I know that experience is that thing you get just an nth of a second after you need it the most. I know you will learn not to pick up the bowl of hot soup without gloves or lift the lid of a rice bowl after making rice in the microwave. When instructions for cooking rice say, *"Let stand for five minutes,"* there's a reason for it. If the server at the restaurant tells you, "Hot plate," well, the plate is hot. Trust them.

I, you, him, her, we can learn it when we're thirty and cooking our first microwave bowl of rice. Or we can learn it at fifty or one hundred. Some things are just true.

To this day, when I whistle, my girls recognize it and come to me. I determined when I was a young mom to not be one of those parents who yell for their children. So, I whistled. Even today, in a crowded mall, (should we ever get to return to one) my girls know their mom's shrill whistle, though aging and lack of use have made the whistle less loud than in its glory days.

Learning the lessons of those who go before us is the essence of living, I think. But, what do I really know? I am the girl who was sneezed on by an elephant at the Asheboro Zoo in the 1970s.

What have you learned the hard way?

What did you warn others about?

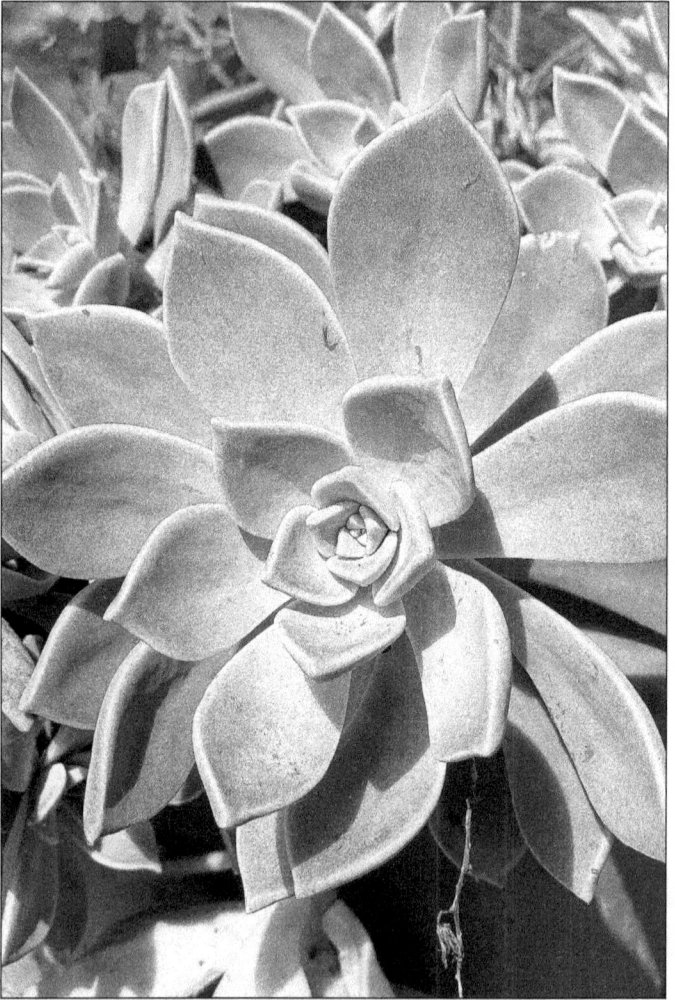

Mother hen and chicks
And on and on they grow.

Love Thy neighbor

There's a portion of my mind that knows the stories in the Bible are not about magic. That stone that killed Goliath? It held no special powers as it came from the little guy and took out the giant. One pebble. One direct hit. Not magic. God directed. But my mind hears the magical.

Jesus and healing the blind, the tormented, the sick. The lame. Making people run when they couldn't walk and had been dependent on the willingness of tired and frustrated friends. I mean, who doesn't get tired of "carrying" a friend?

We can't even carpool with someone who is on our way to work without it getting old. Carry a friend? On a mat? With the help of other friends? Day after day? That act of continuously carrying for the sake of finding the healing is nothing short of a miracle.

Fax machines have supernatural abilities, as far as my brain is concerned. Isn't it magic? Put it in here, take it out there. A little sleight of hand. Make the rabbit reappear.

I believe in the power of the *Night Circus*. The supernatural. The possibilities, the possible. In my soul, with God, opportunities for the magical are endless.

I want to move from the normal, expected, ordinary into the abnormal, paranormal, unexpected, and extraordinary. I do. I agree I may need to rest from the extraordinary, like every seven days or so. But wouldn't it be great to walk through walls? Fly under your own power? Disappear? Reappear? I live an expectant life.

I look to see God at work. And I do—see God at work, that is, in the intersections and algorithms, in the free-flowing streams and crashing waterfalls. God is at work.

I also see God choose not to work. That's where being supernatural is the hardest, I bet. God knows I believe my dad died before I was ready to give him up, for good, while on this earth. But then God also knows I would never willingly give up my dad.

Where's the magic, the miracle, the extraordinary when a person's cancer, once beaten, reoccurs, and it all starts over again? We have each other for as long as we have each other. There's magic in loving your neighbor.

Do you believe in miracles?

How are miracles different from magic?

Gladiolas in Summer
How close must you be to be a neighbor?

French Toast

Do you batter your bread with an egg and fry each side just so? If so, you make what is called French toast. Any bread will do. In fact, banana bread was a favorite of mine for a while. And you can add vanilla and milk, or just a little water and sugar, to the egg batter. Choices abound.

I don't know what I don't know. And I can't do anything about it. I keep learning things and in the learning discover what I don't know, so I can learn more. But there is always more I do not know than that I do.

Such as, where did French toast originate? The obvious take would be France, of course. But not everything that carries a place name is from that place, is it? Burgundy wine, however, should only come from Burgundy. But where does Chardonnay call home?

See that girl over there at the corner table? Her story? She awoke this morning to another bout of back pain. She will ignore it and press on when she should call the doctor. Tomorrow it will be worse. But she doesn't know that today.

Today, she dresses and ties her shoes and visits the bookstore to find a gift for Jackie. And Jackie won't read that book. I know from listening to her telephone call to Carol that she's in pain and she's buying the book. I'm guessing about tomorrow's pain being worse, and about Jackie not reading the book. I don't know what I don't know.

But I have an appetite for research and knowing the answers to questions. I will look up things in a heartbeat. The internet makes it easier than the library used to, when I kept a running list of questions. Thank you, oh great hand-held device. I so appreciate my highly sophisticated piece of wizardry.

I am aware, though, that all that is read may not be right, good, fair, real or true. But that's how I came to be in the library researching French toast. French Toast, by the way, could have been named for the man who served it, a Mr. French, though the dish was served by the ancients as a way to use their leftover bread.

What was the last topic you researched?

What do you think you know, but don't?

At sunrise
Beaufort, North Carolina

Earthquakes in SC

Magnitude: 1.8; Date/Time: 23 June 2014 22:13:53; Location: 33.033N 80.192W; Depth: 10 km... The report goes on. More recently, in 2020, South Carolina had ten from April to June. Our earth frequently shakes. We're a state with faults. Our magnitudes are tiny, but persistent. Magnitude 1.8, 2, 2.2, 3.3...

Once, several years back, my grandmother's sister, Great Aunt Eva Lee, told me about a time she was sitting in a Ladson-area restaurant and jumped when a loud "BOOM" rocked the building and the front glassed windows shook. She said she was sure an eighteen-wheeler had jumped a curb and was heading into the place.

South Carolina's earthquakes are shallow ones. We often hear noise associated with the moving earth, the low-frequency motions of an earthquake's waves, before or as the quake is being felt. Sort of like a knuckle cracking. Does the sound come from the shifting? Before or after it?

Eva Lee lived on the fifth floor of a five-story apartment complex with a Summerville address, too close to the epicenter of the great 1886 quake that rocked Charleston for my comfort. I was always on edge about losing her to another "Great One." I don't have to worry for her safety anymore.

I do, however, continue to worry about the shifting earth and what impact it can have. The scars of the 1886 Charleston/Summerville earthquake are still evident. Homes with bolts defy the shifts. When I left Alaska in 1984, the scars of their "Great Quake" in 1964 were still evident, too. The comedian George Carlin is quoted as saying "The safest place to be during an earthquake would be in a stationary store."

Charles Kuralt, American sojourner and journalist, said, "It takes an earthquake to remind us that we walk on the crust of an unfinished planet."

"All earthquakes and disasters are warnings; there's too much corruption in the world," Aristotle said. Our earth is a faulty one.

We can predict, or have predicted for us, with some reliability, a tornado. Watch the wind in the clouds or the rotation signified by the color purple on a weather app.

We can predict, with some consistency, where the hurricane or typhoon or tsunami will land, and with what force. We can anticipate the amount of rain and snow a storm will bring. We are watchers of the weather because we like to know what is coming. With a small measure of certainty, we understand and know global pandemics attack our health and well-being.

We are joined as a world by the wind. And the waters. And the earth's crust. But we do not know when the earth will jerk upright, shake side-to-side, open chasms, or slide plate over plate. We are knowledgeable, but not that wise.

What we can do is know that while the horrible, the

dreadful, comes, we can steadily plan on, prepare for, and work toward the marvelous and beautiful.

When was the last time you packed a bug-out kit?

Are you as prepared for emergencies as you can be? Or are you over-prepared?

America begins here, with mortar and stone, the website says.
Castillo de San Marcos, St. Augustine, Florida

Cultivating

Delight to the heart,
Joy to the soul.
Lift to the burden.
Making of the whole.

The pipes and strings play the ancient melody
of what was and is and probably will be.

Memories and merry making,
loud smiles on the wind.
Toiling and tending.

Doing it over again.

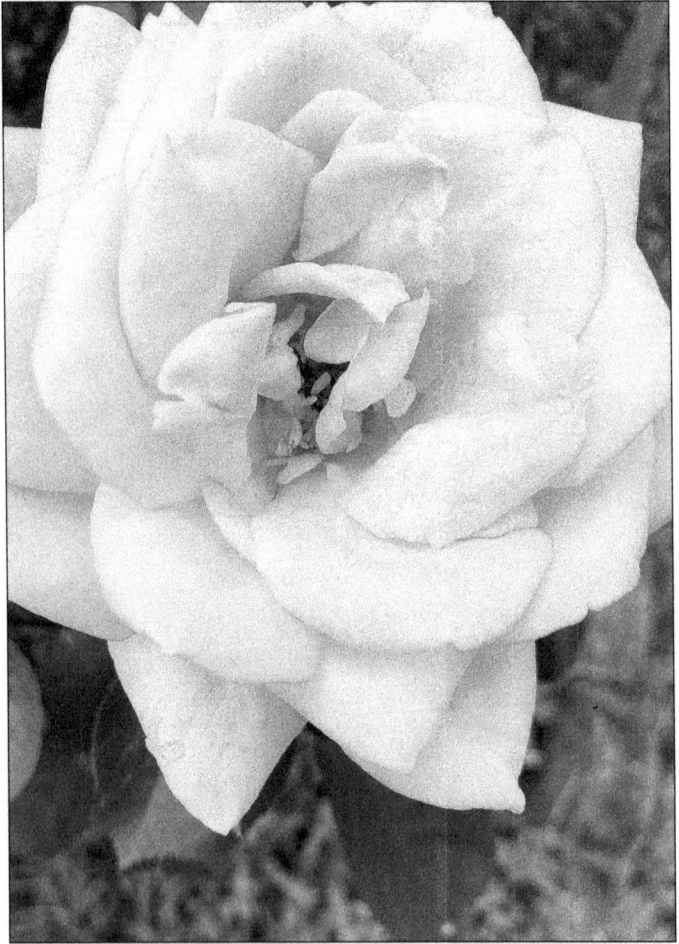

In Bloom

About the Author

Born in Lake City, South Carolina, Dianne Poston Owens is a self-proclaimed philosopher, poet, and wanna-be farmer. She is a veteran print and online journalist, writer, and editor. She works on refining her reflective essays about the nature of the world around her and the humans living in it from her front porch in Hannah, South Carolina. A piece of her flash fiction, *"Crossing the River,"* is online at easystreetmag.com.

Dianne is a wife, mother, grandmother, daughter, sister, and friend. She and husband Dusty live with the other wildlife on a portion of the farm that has been in her family for a hundred years or more. She is active in her DAR chapter and loves studying Colonial America and the American Revolutionary War period. She is a member of the S.C. Press Association.

She reads, writes, and attempts to grow things, some of which are edible. She is a wee bit competitive and loves to play cards and games. After graduating from the University of Alaska, Anchorage, Dianne became a journalist in Georgia and then South Carolina. She has won press awards for her articles. Her first book of essays, *Gathering: Homespun Essays from Beech Tree Lane,* was published in September 2019.

Find her online at www.DianneInHannah.com
Follow her on Twitter @DianneInHannah
Send her an email at Dianne@dianneinhannah.com

www.ingramcontent.com/pod-product-compliance
Lightning Source LLC
Chambersburg PA
CBHW070932030426
42336CB00014BA/2642